# The One Florida Initiative

# The One Florida Initiative

## Reversing Reverse Discrimination

Adriel A. Hilton,
Richard D. Schulterbrandt Gragg III,
Marissa C. Vasquez, and Megan Covington

HAMILTON BOOKS
*Lanham • Boulder • New York • London*

Published by Hamilton Books
An imprint of The Rowman & Littlefield Publishing Group, Inc.
4501 Forbes Boulevard, Suite 200, Lanham, Maryland 20706
www.rowman.com

6 Tinworth Street, London SE11 5AL, United Kingdom



British Library Cataloguing in Publication Information Available

**Library of Congress Control Number:**

Library of Congress Control Number: 2021932121

ISBN: 978-0-7618-7276-4 (cloth)
ISBN: 978-0-7618-7277-1 (electronic)

## Dedication

This book is dedicated to those scholars, advocates, and mentors who strive to create inclusive spaces and to produce quality research that challenges the status quo.

Dr. Adriel A. Hilton

This book is dedicated to those who are closest to me: my parents, Alphonso and Sarah Hilton, Jr.; my sister, Shaquaelia Q. Blanding; and my beautiful niece, Sarah Nicole Penn. Had it not been for your support, sacrifice, guidance, and unwavering love, I would not have been able to accomplish this goal.

My deepest appreciate goes to my late Uncle Alvertis Hilton, for his superb guidance and wise counsel. His leadership and support have enhanced me intellectually and morally.

Dr. Richard D. Gragg, III

My contribution to this book is dedicated to the late Brother Rodderick L. Moorer (11.29.1950–10.29.2014). 'Brother Rodd' was a passionate teacher, dedicated mentor and faithful friend. He taught American Government and Economics for Leon County Schools at the School for Applied and Individual Learning in Tallahassee, Florida. He excelled in this role for thirty years teaching, inspiring and transforming future generations of legal scholars and practitioners.

# Contents

# Tables

# Foreword

## *From One Florida to One Nation*

In this sixty-fourth anniversary year of the groundbreaking Supreme Court decision in the *Brown v. Board of Education* case that outlawed segregation in the nation's public schools, new research reveals that schools have undergone significant re-segregation. The anguish that many of us feel about this incredible failure of public policy underscores the layered aspect of achieving racial equality in America. Moreover, it is juxtaposed against the satisfaction created by the hugely unexpected realization that an African American family recently resided at the most important address in the world: 1600 Pennsylvania Avenue in Washington, D.C. Such is the state of affairs in the United States of America at this point in time where matters related to race are concerned—situations, usually complicated, often confusing, and frequently unsettling to some segments of the population.

School attendance today is largely determined by residential patterns and economic class. Neighborhood racial homogeneity is prevalent across the country, which allows one to fairly and accurately predict that public school systems in urban areas will be attended almost entirely by African American and Hispanic children, while those in suburban communities will have overwhelmingly White enrollments. In the higher education community, the issue of racial and cultural representation is a bit more nuanced than it is in the K–12 system. From a theoretical standpoint, there is a general (though certainly not unanimous) sentiment that achieving racial and ethnic diversity in postsecondary institutions has a positive value. In practice, however, political considerations create a very complicated set of circumstances where efforts to increase enrollment of students of color are concerned.

Florida provides quite an interesting backdrop for discussions and analyses regarding diversity in higher education. Hilton and colleagues recognize that the changing face of higher education and the realization of the demographic data is a vital consideration if Florida is to remain true to its mission of serving the residents of the state and preparing its students for the workplace. U.S. Census Bureau data show that minorities represent the fastest growing population groups in Florida during the last decade. Further, population increases in Florida resulted in projections that with the current rate of growth, the state would become the third largest in the nation in the very near future, perhaps as early as 2011. Notwithstanding the changes in the state's demography, public institutions of higher education in Florida appear to have widened, rather than narrowed, the enrollment gap between the majority and minority populations.

In Florida, and across the nation, the steps that have been taken to implement affirmative action in higher education have been under constant attack by conservatives, and a series of actions by various state and federal courts have resulted in reduced access and enrollment of students of color in several states. Governor Jeb Bush used his authority to redefine affirmative action in his state by issuing an executive order that established the One Florida Initiative (OFI). Bush's claim that the OFI was intended to increase diversity and opportunities for people of color in Florida's State University System appears to be contradicted by findings that minority representation actually decreased in most of the state universities after the policy was implemented.

Hilton and colleagues have provided a cogent analysis of the effects of the OFI on enrollment patterns in the state's public law schools to help us understand how changes in public policy can have detrimental effects on particular communities. The research is both enriched and complicated by the inclusion of the two law schools at Florida A&M and Florida International Universities, which are both minority serving institutions. These schools were developed independently of the OFI but had a potential effect on the level of diversity that can be calculated across the system. The use of critical race theory offers an approach that will prove unnerving to some readers, but is one that provided insights that may not have been revealed through a different framework.

The shift from the use of affirmative action practices to the race neutral approach of OFI was ostensibly done to increase diversity in the law schools. As a result of OFI and the two law schools at Florida A&M University and Florida International University, the data show that minority student enrollment in the state's public law schools increased. Using critical race theory, Hilton and colleagues accept the proposition that the two phenomena were intended to improve diversity. I am less certain of that intended outcome. Coupled with the operation of the two law schools at the minority serving institutions, the implementation of OFI resulted in an increase in the representation of African Americans and Latinos in Florida. Still, White students were the group who benefitted most from this policy change because their opportunities to attend law schools in Florida were expanded.

Recent articles in *The American Lawyer* point out that "the paucity of minority students in law schools has been the source of hand-wringing for decades, not only by legal educators but also by advocates who recognize that the larger legal profession can't diversify unless law schools do so first." Nevertheless, the American Bar Association statistics show only modest gains in this arena during the past decade. "That means legal education has a long way to go before it reflects the diversity of the country as a whole, considering that minorities made up 37 percent of the population in 2012." In this regard, law schools are emblematic of the larger American society and the ongoing contradictions between its ideals and its practices. Even while the continued existence of racism, discrimination, intolerance, and injustice are repeatedly confirmed in surveys conducted by both governmental and private agencies, resistance to change on the part of the majority population is manifested in the unwillingness to relinquish the benefits of structurally implanted racial privilege.

Perhaps the confluence of the OFI and the opening of law schools at two minority serving institutions of higher education present a template that can be used in other circumstances and localities. Recognizing that the expansion of communities of color will be the basis for the continuing growth of Florida's population, this situation may provide the opportunity for visionary public officials of that state to open additional law schools in conjunction with other Historically Black Institutions such as Bethune-Cookman College or Edward Waters College. While these colleges are private, the operation of public-private partnerships has long been one of the approaches that conservatives have advocated to achieve responsive government and effective delivery of important services to communities. Nationally, the percentage of African American law students has stagnated during the past decade, and while Hispanic students are still underrepresented, their enrollment has increased by almost fifty percent during this period. Opening additional law schools at Historically Black Colleges and Universities—institutions that have proven their value and effectiveness over time—would seem to be a reasonable approach to addressing a problem that has significant social and economic consequences.

If we presume, for argument's sake, that greater representation of people of color in such important fields as law, medicine and the STEM fields is important, and we acknowledge that additional opportunities for members of these groups would benefit the nation as a whole, then the situation analyzed by Hilton and colleagues could well be expanded. If the political winds continue to blow towards the implementation of race-neutral admission policies to professional schools, then why not complement those policies with new programs in institutions that have demonstrated their historical capability to educate underrepresented populations? In Florida, that could mean a School of Medicine and a School of Computer Technology at Florida A&M. Clearly, the minority serving law schools in the state have shown their capacity to attract White students in a way that the majority law schools are unable to achieve for African American and Hispanic students. It seems reasonable to conclude then, that new professional schools at MSIs will benefit not just members of minority groups, but all Floridians.

Further, this concept can be extended outside Florida. Historically Black Colleges and Universities in Maryland, for example, have recently won a court case that upheld their claim of historical disparate treatment compared to predominantly White institutions of higher education. Why then should the state of Maryland not take this opportunity to establish a medical school at Bowie State University, a law school at Morgan State University, and a school of agriculture at the University of Maryland-Eastern Shore? Wouldn't the citizens of Mississippi benefit from a medical school at Mississippi Valley State University, a law school at Alcorn State University, and a school of nanoscience at Jackson State University? This suggested pattern of institutional enhancement for minority serving institutions, capitalizing on the strengths of colleges and universities across the nation, could be projected across the Southeast and the Southwest, where large portions of the African American and Hispanic populations are located.

Hilton and colleagues' analysis of the One Florida Initiative has opened the doors to our imagination by revealing the provision of additional opportunities for people of color achieved through the law schools at Florida A&M and Florida International Universities. Given the stark levels of political polarization and societal division across the country, perhaps movement towards one nation would be enhanced by developing real additional opportunities for underserved populations, not in the false promise of race-neutral approaches alone, but rather in the creation of new opportunities built on the foundation of proven institutional structures.

William B. Harvey
Rector, Danubius University

# Acknowledgments

First and foremost, we would like to acknowledge our publisher, Hamilton Books. We are grateful for the support to seeing this project to fruition. Collectively, we would like to acknowledge the book contributors who made this text possible. These wonderful researchers include: Drs. William B. Harvey and John T. Wolfe, Jr. We appreciate your commitment to these issues.

# Introduction

The demographic face of higher education in the United States is changing and will continue to do so in the foreseeable future. According to the US Census Bureau (2010), minorities in the last decade represented the fastest growing populations in states like California, Florida, and Texas. This trend is projected to continue at an even faster pace over the next two to three decades in what might reasonably be called a population explosion. As a result, colleges and universities, including community colleges, are becoming increasingly focused on racial and ethnic diversity. For institutions of higher education in the states of California, Texas, Washington, Michigan, and Florida, such focus will be vital if they are to remain true to their missions of serving the residents of their states and preparing their undergraduate, graduate, and professional students for the global marketplace. In Florida, 30.6 percent of Black and 48.5 percent of Latino students are enrolled in the State University System (SUS) and the state college system combined (State University System of Florida, 2011; Florida Department of Education, 2013). With such trends projected to increase, institutions of higher education must prepare for a more ethnically and racially diverse society to adequately equip future generations to meet the inevitable social, political, and economic opportunities and challenges. As of now, Florida appears to be ill-prepared for the new diversity, based on decisions and policies implemented during the early part of the last decade, in particular, the One Florida Initiative (OFI). The OFI sought to increase diversity in education within the state by revising race-based admissions practices and contract set-asides. However, rather than becoming more diverse, Florida's public education system, including its law schools, has widened the gap between minorities and the majority population in the makeup of their student bodies ("Jeb Bush's One," 2006).

Implemented in 1999 by the state's Republican Governor, John Ellis "Jeb" Bush and Lieutenant Governor Frank Brogan, the OFI (also referred to as Executive Order 99–281) was designed to transcend traditional notions of affirmative action (Klink, 2003; Orfield & Miller, 1998; Rivers, 2000). Affirmative action, a policy stemming from the Civil Rights Act of 1964, is designed to provide equitable access to minorities who are often overlooked for employment and educational opportunities (Connor, 1985). The OFI was established with the intent to unite Floridians with a shared vision. Its purpose was to increase opportunities and diversity in the SUS of Florida, as well as in government employment and state contracting, by turning a blind-eye to race and ethnicity. According to Governor Bush, "The OFI is diversity without quotas, preferences, or set-asides and it was designated not to abandon affirmative action, but to substantively redefine it" (Bush, 2000, p.1). The executive order prohibits the use of affirmative action in Florida's school admissions policies in an effort to "support equal educational opportunities for all qualified Floridians, to prohibit discrimination in education because of race, gender, creed, color or national origin" (Florida Department of Management Services, 1999).

Yet despite its intent, the percentage of minority student enrollment, particularly that of African American students, declined within the SUS of Florida upon implementation of the OFI. For example, prior to its enactment, African American and Latino students each represented 14 percent of the student population in the SUS, respectively (SUSF, 2014). Post OFI, enrollment trends of African American students remained constant at 14 percent in the years 2000–2002. In 2003, the SUS saw an increase of 1 percent (a total of 15 percent) of this student population. However, the representation of Black students declined once again in 2004 at 14 percent. This minor fluctuation continued over the next seven years (2005–2011), yet dipped once more to 13 percent in the years 2012 and 2013 (SUSF, 2014). For Latinos, enrollment trends after the implementation of OFI has steadily increased; yet the representation of these students within the entire SUS of Florida was still less than 25 percent in 2013 (SUSF, 2014).

While affirmative action was designed to overcome the remnants of historically rooted discrimination, this policy exists now in many different forms as a result of an almost constant legal attack by opponents who argue that it amounts to reverse discrimination against Whites (Connor, 1985). Conservatives also view affirmative action as a policy that encourages complacency among minorities and promotes a sense of low self-esteem in those who participate (Delgado, 1995). As such, proponents of the conservative viewpoint argue for a meritorious system of employment practices that relies more heavily on an applicant's job skills and knowledge. These proponents argue that meritocracy promotes the hiring of employees based on their knowledge, skills, and abilities rather than political connections, race, or social policies. Thus, anti-affirmative action proponents claim that the best way to remedy past practices of exclusion is to dismiss affirmative action efforts and practice inclusion of all individuals, regardless of race (Delgado, 1995).

Court challenges to minority set-asides, commonly found in many affirmative action programs, have been initiated in several states by citizens ranging from business owners bidding on government contracts to medical and law school applicants. For example, Supreme Court decisions during the 1970s through the 1990s significantly diluted affirmative action programs (Milakovich & Gordon, 2001). One notable case involved a White man who had applied to medical school at the University of California at Davis. Allan Bakke had been rejected twice by the admissions officers, although he considered himself more qualified than some of the minorities who had been admitted. In 1978, Bakke argued successfully that the medical school's quota for admitting minorities amounted to reverse discrimination. The U.S. Supreme Court agreed and ordered Bakke to be admitted (*University of California Regents v. Bakke*, 1978). In a more recent case, the United States Supreme Court issued a ruling in *Fisher v. University of Texas* (2014), which again was directed towards a university's college admission affirmative action policy. Abigail Noel Fisher individually sued the flagship state university, University of Texas at Austin, after her freshman college application was denied in Fall 2008. Fisher argued that the University of Texas's use of race in admissions decisions violated her right to equal protection under the Fourteenth Amendment, claiming that she had been treated differently than some less-qualified minority students who were accepted. After the United States District Court upheld the legality of the university's admission policy, the plaintiff sought further review from the U.S. Supreme Court. In June 2013, the Supreme Court offered an indirect ruling on the program's constitutionality by ordering further scrutiny by the 5th U.S. Circuit District Court of Appeals. On July 15, 2014, the panel voted 2–1 and ruled in favor of the University of Texas, stating that the university had justified its limited use of race to achieve diversity, given a lack of workable alternatives.

As a result of legal challenges, affirmative action programs have evolved several times over the years, from a policy to protect minorities and women to one that assists anyone considered disadvantaged without regard to race or gender. The courts, in allowing such challenges to affirmative action to prevail, ignore the evidence that suggests that race is indeed a factor not to be overlooked as a means for increasing minority enrollment in colleges and universities (Orfield & Miller, 1998).

## THE ROLE OF MINORITY SERVING INSTITUTIONS

In an effort to address such inequities, colleges and universities have been established to serve specific needs of students of color. In the last two decades, the number of minority-serving institutions (MSIs), including historically Black colleges and universities (HBCUs), Hispanic-serving institutions (HSIs), tribal colleges and universities (TCUs), and Asian American and Native American Pacific Islander Serving Institutions (AANAPISIs) has grown by 200 percent (Gasman, 2009). These institutions educate more than 2.3 million collegians (13 percent), with the majority being students of color. Historically, HBCUs have played a critical role in the American higher education system. Although not officially recognized by Congress until 1965, HBCUs were established long before then. Institutions such as Cheyney University of Pennsylvania (1837), Lincoln University (1854), and Wilberforce University (1856) were some of the first HBCUs founded prior to the American Civil War. However, it was not until the enactment of Title III of the Higher Education Act of 1965 that the United States Congress officially defined an HBCU as an accredited school of higher learning whose principal mission was the education of African Americans. While HBCU's currently represent 3 percent of all colleges and universities, they enroll 16 percent of the nation's undergraduate African American students.

The emergence of HSIs came as a result of organic demographic shifts and growth of the Latino population within the educational pipeline. As more Latino students navigated through PreK–12, post-secondary institutions saw a steady influx of these students at its doors. As a result, an amendment to Title V, Part A of the Higher Education Act was made in an effort to ". . . expand educational opportunities for, and improve the attainment of, Hispanic students" (U.S. Department of Education, n.d.-c). Designated HSIs are awarded grants intended to enable such colleges and universities opportunities to expand and enhance their academic offerings, program quality, and institutional stability. In order for an institution to be federally designated as an HSI, a minimum of 25 percent of its student population must be Latino, with no less than 50 percent of its students being eligible for need-based assistance (HACU, 2014). Thus, while not initially established to serve Latino students exclusively, Hispanic-serving institutions have become increasingly significant as they enroll more than 42 percent of all Latino students in the United States.

In 1968, the Navajo nation founded the first tribal college, Navajo Community College (later renamed Diné College), in Arizona. As of today, there are 34 accredited tribal colleges and universities in the United States. Stemming from Native American activism during the late 1960s and the Indian Self-De-termination and Educational Assistance Act of 1975, these institutions serve more than 30,000 full and part-time students at campuses located primarily in the Midwest and Southwestern United States. As of 2013, American Indian and Alaskan Native students represented 78 percent of the total enrollment at these institutions. However, despite federal recognition, tribal colleges and universities remain underfunded and are often the only options for postsecondary education for students from poor rural communities. Until 2007, no federal legislation existed concerning Asian American and Native American Pacific Islander-Serving Institutions (AANAPISI). Originally authorized by the College Cost Reduction and Access Act of 2007, federally designated AANAPISIs are eligible for federal grant funding. Similar to HSIs, institutions in which Asian Americans and Pacific Islander students constitute at least 25 percent of the total undergraduate enrollment may apply for designation status.

While these MSIs serve a substantial population of undergraduate students in the country, many are also committed to preparing students of color in graduate programs and professional schools. Howard University, for example, was the first HBCU to establish a law school dedicated to training Black lawyers (Howard University, 2006). Chartered in 1869, the mission of Howard University School of Law is to provide a legal education to those who have been excluded from the profession of law by providing them with ". . .the professional leadership necessary to advocate and defend the rights of all, but particularly of African Americans and other minorities" (Howard University, 2006). The 1940s saw a proliferation of MSI graduate and professional schools as a result of court cases brought forward by Blacks who had been turned away from graduate programs at all White public universities (Gannon, 1996; Rivers, 2000). Some of these decisions (*Hawkins v. Board of Control*, 1950; *Sweatt v. Painter*, 1950) had a profound effect on opportunities for Blacks to obtain a graduate and professional education, legal and otherwise. For example, in North Carolina, the enactment of House Bill 18 on March 1, 1939 by the State's General Assembly ". . .paved the way for a new generation of African American lawyers" (North Carolina Central University, 2007). The bill authorized a law school to be opened at North Carolina Central University, which became the only in-state option for Blacks to receive a legal education.

In Florida, the path toward equal opportunities for Black Americans to attend public law school in the state was prompted in 1949, when Virgil Darnell Hawkins was denied admission to the University of Florida (UF) College of Law based solely upon race. Hawkins took his case to the Florida Supreme Court, who suggested that he attend the Florida Agricultural and Mechanical University (FAMU) College of Law, an all-Black law school ordered by the state as a way to avoid integration. While Hawkins declined the offer, FAMU moved forth in admitting its first class in 1951. However, in 1965 Florida legislature voted to close the FAMU's School of Law and transfer supporting funds to the newly established law school at Florida State University (FSU), a predominantly White institution (Rivers, 2000). It was not until the year 2000, thirty-five years later, that a coalition of state legislators introduced bills to reinstate FAMU's law school and establish the Florida International University (FIU) College of Law.

While it has been more than 30 years since the implementation of the OFI, and nearly 15 years since the establishment of Florida's two new MSI law schools, some might argue that not much has changed. Although the intent of the OFI was to increase access to higher education for Black students throughout the state's postsecondary education systems, previously outlined enrollment data indicates otherwise. As such, the representation of Black students in Florida's public law schools has also remained stagnant.

## STATEMENT OF THE PROBLEM

Minorities are underrepresented in Florida's legal profession as a result of a lack of access, enrollment, and production of minorities from publicly supported law schools (Herbert, 1999). As previously noted, while the OFI promised greater diversity within the SUS of Florida, data have demonstrated that schools are in fact more segregated following the OFI (Marin & Lee, 2003; Orfield & Miller, 1998). Very few studies have examined the impact of the OFI and the creation of two MSI law schools, namely FAMU College of Law and FIU College of Law (which occurred independently of the OFI), on increasing diversity in Florida's public law schools. There is also little research concerning the impact of these changes on the production of minorities for Florida's legal profession. It is also unclear what impact these new law schools have had on minority enrollment at the existing predominately White institutions that comprise the SUS of Florida. This study contributes to the availability of pertinent research on the impact of policies based on affirmative action as traditionally defined.

The purpose of this study was to gain an understanding of the impact made by the OFI and MSI law schools on diversity within Florida's legal profession. Specifically, this research sought the perceptions of six administrators from three law schools in the state of Florida. These administrators consisted of law school deans and admissions personnel. Participants were asked to share their views on the impact of Governor Bush's executive order on (a) diversity within the SUS of Florida law schools, and (b) the impact of the two newly established MSI law schools on the mission statements, recruitment efforts and admission practices after implementation of the OFI.

## SIGNIFICANCE OF THE STUDY

This study investigated the effects of a public policy change in the state of Florida, namely the OFI. As a result of changing demographics across the country, colleges and universities are enhancing their focus and efforts towards serving a more diverse student population. Such service is important, as there is a need to not only educate, but also prepare the next generation of professionals to compete in the national workforce. In an effort to meet this goal, institutions, including those in the state of Florida, have reexamined admission and recruitment practices to ensure that their commitment to diversity is maintained. Yet while these practices appear philosophically sound (i.e., serving all students regardless of race/ethnicity), they also lead to the dilution of affirmative action policies that seek to promote social justice and equality to those who are unfairly disadvantaged.

Given the dearth of literature regarding the effects of race-neutral policies, specifically the OFI, on the enrollment of minority students in Florida's law schools, the present study was of much importance. As more states become targeted for future affirmative action policy changes, this study sought to provide policy makers and voters insight into the likely impact of their actions. The work presented serves as a primary research methodology for others to examine in the future, as well as provides valuable information to institutions seeking diversity in their law school enrollment.

The results of this study are important for several reasons; not least among them is the benefit to others who are interested in the subject of diversity in higher education. It may also encourage other researchers to look further into the impact that implementation of non-traditional affirmative action models might have on other communities considering similar initiatives. This study may be helpful to those interested in developing policies and models that seek to increase diversity on their campuses, as well as to those seeking to make informed decisions about policies affecting the use of conventional affirmative action. It was anticipated that the findings of this study would (a) contribute to the literature on affirmative action in Florida, and (b) assist the SUS in improving affirmative action related policies. The dearth of existing research in the literature about this subject inhibits the ability of many citizens and lawmakers to reach rational and informed conclusions when faced with decisions about affirmative action.

This book seeks to provide a greater access to scholarly research beyond the academic community. It is also intended to provide a power of speech to those who are silenced by the lack of adequate information in the literature on this subject. By advancing the outcomes found in this study, the wealth of knowledge available about this issue will be increased, hopefully leading to better policies and practices towards achieving racial and ethnic diversity in law school enrollment, graduation rates, and the profession in America.

# *Chapter One*

# Emergence of Affirmative Action

Despite the advances for underserved students in higher education via court rulings such as *Brown v. Board of Education of Topeka* (1954), it would take more to erase the past mistreatment of minorities in the United States. President Lyndon B. Johnson attempted to address that when he implemented a policy he called "affirmative action" on July 2, 1964. President Johnson's Executive Order 11246 (1965), and later Executive Order 11748 (1969), mandated that federal government offices and companies doing business with the federal government promote equality to ensure that minorities and women were integrated in government jobs at the federal, state, and local levels. The mandate forced employers to prove that they had taken affirmative steps to promote opportunities for minorities and women (Starling, 2002, p. 48). Affirmative action programs at the federal level succeeded in increasing the representation of women and Latino males in certain managerial positions. Based on 2016 U.S. Census data, 51.5 percent of managerial positions were occupied by women and 9.1 percent by African Americans. In 2002, 21 percent of women, 17 percent of African American women, and 13 percent of African American men undertook managerial positions, compared to 19 percent of Whites (U.S. Bureau of the Census 2002, p. 1). In addition, Reskin (1998) noted that due to affirmative action, the pay gap between publicly employed Latinos and women decreased when compared to their White male colleagues. For many, affirmative action has provided opportunities to ensure that underrepresented groups be given fair and equitable treatment. The policy includes outreach programs targeted at specific groups that have been historically subordinated by notifying them of employment and contracting opportunities. This policy was not only implemented in higher education, but also in government agencies and corporate America, which led it to becoming an immediate target for litigation in the nation's courts.

The first significant challenge to affirmative action in the U.S. was initiated in 1971 and went as far as the Supreme Court. Black employees of Duke Power Company in North Carolina filed suit against the company, claiming they were being subjected to racial discrimination (*Griggs v. Duke Power Co*., 1971). Their claim was based on Duke Power's educational requirements and tests administered to those wishing to be hired or promoted within the company, which had no apparent relationship to an employee's ability to perform the job. The plaintiffs charged that the tests, as well as the requirement for a high school diploma or college degree, amounted to racial selectivity. The Court found that requiring certain education levels and tests to measure basic skills was, in fact, legal. It ruled, however, that such criteria could not be used to qualify or disqualify any individual for employment or advancement based on his or her race (*Griggs v. Duke Power Co*., 1971):

> The facts of this case demonstrate the inadequacy of broad and general testing devices as well as the infirmity of using diplomas or degrees as fixed measures of capability. History is filled with examples of men and women who rendered highly effective performance without the conventional badges of accomplishment in terms of certificates, diplomas, or degrees. Diplomas and tests are useful servants, but Congress has mandated the commonsense proposition that they are not to become masters of reality. (Burger, 1972)

In 1978, the first landmark educational test of affirmative action was brought forth in the case of *University of California Regents v. Bakke* (1978). Bakke's suit challenged the constitutionality of admission policies by the University of California at Davis (UCD) Medical School, which included a dual admissions program; one for regular admits, in keeping with the school's normal requirements, and another for minority or "disadvantaged" students. The plaintiff in this case (Bakke, a White male) had twice been rejected from UCD's medical school despite having a high qualification score. In each case, according to the suit, students in the disadvantaged or minority group were admitted with lower overall scores than Bakke. He sued claiming a violation of his constitutional right to equal protection under the law. Bakke prevailed and was eventually granted admission to the school. The majority opinion of the U.S. Supreme Court stated:

> In summary, it is evident that the Davis special admissions program involves the use of an explicit racial classification never before countenanced by this Court. It tells applicants who are not Negro, Asian, or Chicano that they are totally excluded from a specific percentage of the seats in an entering class. No matter how strong their qualifications, quantitative and extracurricular, including their own potential for contribution to educational diversity, they are never afforded

> the chance to compete with applicants from the preferred groups for the special admissions seats. (Powell, 1978)

The ruling was widely denounced by civil rights activists at the time as a setback to the future of affirmative action. The future of affirmative action was, in fact, held in question given the continued attacks on the practice, legal and otherwise, in virtually all segments of public policy.

The case of *Hopwood v. State of Texas* is one example of the continued legal battles over affirmative action. In this 1992 case, four White citizens were denied admission to the University of Texas School of Law. The suit claimed that their denial came as a result of the school's special race-sensitive criteria for certain applicants. The plaintiffs claimed that the policy in question was discriminatory because it gave African Americans and Mexican Americans preference for admittance, which inflicted harm to Whites and others. The Fifth U.S. Circuit Court of Appeals was asked to decide whether the 14th Amendment permitted the University of Texas law school to show preference to any one group or groups. Their decision was stated as follows:

> We hold that it does not. The law school has presented no compelling justification, under the Fourteenth Amendment or Supreme Court precedent, that allows it to continue to elevate some races over others, even for the wholesome purpose of correcting perceived racial imbalance in the student body. (*Hopwood v. State of Texas*, 1996)

The decision, however, was not a complete victory for the four plaintiffs as the court only granted a minimal amount of money to each of them for damages and forced the law school to simply allow the plaintiffs to apply again without paying the required application fee. The court did not ban the law school from using race in its admission decisions in the future (*Hopwood v. State of Texas*, 1996). Nearly 20 years later, a similar ruling was issued in *Fisher v. Texas* (2015), which stated that race-conscious admission practices could be used at the University of Texas at Austin for the purpose of ensuring a diverse student body (*Fisher v. Texas*, 2016).

While some states continued to debate the pros and cons of affirmative action, the U.S. Supreme Court continued to hear more cases involving the policy. In 2003, two cases in one state were decided when the high court heard arguments in *Gratz v. Bollinger* and *Grutter v. Bollinger*, both suing the University of Michigan. In these cases, the plaintiffs claimed the University of Michigan extended unfair advantages to Blacks and other minorities over Whites with regard to the school's admission practices. In the *Gratz v. Bollinger* case, the Court ruled that the use of race in making undergraduate admission decisions was a violation of the equal protection clause and Title

VI of the Constitution. In the *Grutter v. Bollinger* case, however, the Court's decision allowed the law school to continue using race in its admission decisions because of what the Court termed a compelling interest in diversifying its student body for educational purposes.

Affirmative action in government contract awards was dealt a similar setback in 1988, when it was ruled that the City of Richmond, Virginia's program to benefit minority businesses violated the rights of private contractors (*City of Richmond v. J.A. Croson Co.*, 1989). The plan mandated that 30 percent of all subcontracts be given to companies owned by minorities. Yet this plan was declared unconstitutional because the city failed to prove that the program was in the public's interest. In 1995, another case by Adarand Constructors, Inc. raised questions about federal minority preference programs (*Adarand Constructors v. Peña*, 1995). The primary issue in the case centered on U.S. Transportation Secretary Federico Peña's federal highway project, which, according to the plaintiffs, favored disadvantaged business owners. In 2002, another high-profile reverse discrimination charge was filed in the case *Biondi v. City of Chicago.* In an effort to promote minorities through the command ranks of the Chicago Fire Department, the City of Chicago adjusted the test scores of minorities on the 1986 lieutenant's promotional test (Stowell, 2002, p. 30). Ten White men charged that the city's pursuit of diversity cost them promotions, despite their hard work. They argued that the City of Chicago's actions amounted to a denial of firefighters' rights under Title VII of the Civil Rights Act of 1964. The ten plaintiffs won the case and were awarded a total of $2.6 million in damages.

Such cases, both in and out of the higher education arena, underscore our nation's divide over the issue of affirmative action. Over the years, the number of states adopting anti-affirmative action policies has increased. In 1996, California voters approved Proposition 209, a referendum abolishing preferential treatment based on gender or race in public hiring and educational admission (Milakovich & Gordon, 2001). The 54 percent assenting vote was noted as a backlash against affirmative action aimed at Blacks, Hispanics, immigrants, and women. The Federal Appeals Court upheld the California decision, spreading the incentives for others in neighboring states to take on similar policies. In 1998, voters in the state of Washington passed a similar ballot measure entitled "Initiative 200," which also repealed affirmative action programs in public employment, education, and contracting. The state of Florida followed suit one year later via the Governor's Executive Order 99-281, 1999, known as the One Florida Initiative (OFI). Amid considerable controversy, Florida abolished preferential treatment for minorities in an effort to increase diversity and opportunities without using discriminatory policies.

The anti-affirmative action policies established in two of these three states came as a result of citizen participation and changing voter demographics. For example, in California, Latinos (ironically) had the highest voter turnout of those in favor of Proposition 209. Support for Washington's Initiative 200 was garnered by campaigns encouraging voters to reduce discrimination against qualified White males in city, county, and state governments. While the two state laws and Florida's executive order claim to be non-discriminatory initiatives, they have in fact dismantled their state's affirmative action programs.

## MINORITY REPRESENTATION IN FLORIDA'S LAW SCHOOLS

Despite efforts over the past forty years intended to increase diversity in the nation's law schools, such as affirmative action and quota systems, minority enrollment in majority institutions remains stubbornly low compared to Whites. After the implementation of the OFI, which banned the use of race or gender in admission decisions for undergraduate and graduate programs, Black student enrollment in two of Florida's most prominent law schools declined (*Journal of Blacks in Education*, 2006). Black enrollment diminished notably at the University of Florida (UF) College of Law. In 2000, there were 53 Black students in the entering class; however, by 2004 the number fell to 22, a decrease of more than half (*Journal of Blacks in Higher Education*, 2006). In 2005, the enrollment of Black first-year students was approximately 35—making the number of Black students still 34 percent below the level which existed prior to the OFI. Florida State University (FSU) College of Law also experienced a decline in Black enrollment. In 2000, the College of Law enrolled 23 Black students in its entering class; however, in 2005 only ten Black law students were enrolled in the first-year class (*Journal of Blacks in Higher Education*, 2006).

Many would argue that the early gains of affirmative action have been wiped out by a lack of widespread adherence to this policy or as a result of other policies that lessen the chances of minorities to successfully gain admittance to law school and in higher education in general (Antonovics & Backes, 2014; Bowen & Bok, 2016; Heriot, 2015; Long, 2015a; Long, 2015b). Ashkenas, Park, and Pearce (2017) use a New York Times analysis to note that even with affirmative action, Blacks and Hispanics remain more underrepresented in top universities than thirty-five years ago. According to the American Bar Association (ABA), the number of applicants to law schools, public and private, for the years 2013–2014 rose dramatically for minority students. However, the increase in applications did not translate into a similar rise in the number of admits for Black students.

Data from the ABA show an increase of nearly 25,000 applications to law schools around the nation between the base year of 1995 and the peak year of 2004. Who accounted for the majority of the increase? White applicants were responsible for much of the increase with over 12,000 more applications during 2004, compared with 1995, followed by Asians, Hispanics, and African American applicants, respectively. While the number of law school applicants admitted rose by about 5,000, the groups accounting for nearly all of the 5,000 new slots for law schools were Asian, White, and Hispanic. The number of African American applicants admitted into law schools remained static, and actually dropped slightly over the ten-year period. Based on the 2016 Law School Admission Council data, 4,760 Black law school applicants were admitted for fall 2014 and 4,680 were admitted for fall 2015. This was a 7.2 percent decrease (ABA, 2006). These statistics should not be interpreted as an indication that African Americans are not able to do the work required for success in law school. Randall (2004) discovered that it is more discrimination than lack of ability.

> Randall (2006) determined that the use of the Law School Admission Test (LSAT) as the sole determining factor in admission, specifically with its cut-off score, is an example of institutional racism. Specifically, it is estimated that at least 90 percent of law schools have admission practices that presumptively deny applicants based on how they fall on a grid formulated around LSAT and Undergraduate Grade Point Average (UGPA). It is the misuse of the LSAT that has a discriminatory impact (Randall, 2004; Randall, 2006).

These challenges and others will continue to charge the debate of whether affirmative action amounts to reverse discrimination against the White majority or equal treatment of racial and ethnic minorities.

# *Chapter Two*

# Theoretical Framework and Context

The theoretical framework for analysis of the OFI is through the transdisciplinary lens of Critical Race Theory (Taylor, 1999; Ladson-Billings, 1998; Ladson-Billings & Tate, 1995). Critical Race Theory (CRT) argues that Whites have been the primary beneficiaries of civil and political rights legislation, rules, and public policies, such as those connected to affirmative action, that ultimately support the status quo of White authority and its subordination of people of color in America. Critical race theorists' interests are grounded in the study and transformation of the relationship among race, racism, and power (Delgado & Stefancic, 1995; Delgago & Stefancic, 2012). One objective is to break the bond that exists between law and racial power (Delgado & Stefancic, 1995; Taylor, 1999; Ladson-Billings, 1998). It is within this framework that critical race theorists Bell, Delgado, Crenshaw, Solorzano, Yosso, and others examine the legal, constitutional, and civil rights concerns, including affirmative action, in the contexts of the associations between White power and law (Daye et al., 2012; Crenshaw, 2011; Solorzano & Yosso, 2002; Calmore, 1993). Therefore, and on many fronts, the impacts of the OFI on the SUS of Florida law schools lends itself to the analytical rubric of CRT.

With roots in critical legal studies, CRT examines the intersection of race, law and power based on the following set of six assumptions: 1]. Storytelling is a significant part of the law. Evidence suggests that the disenfranchised have different stories and different ways of telling them than do the enfranchised (Dickinson, 2012; Connerly 2007; Solorzano & Yosso, 2002; Aguirre, 2000; Delgado & Stefancic, 1995; Crenshaw et al., 1995); 2]. Racist behavior is not an aberration or rare occurrence; it is normal practice (Solorzano, Ceja & Yosso, 2000; Delgado & Stefancic, 1995; Mills, 1997; Crenshaw et al., 1995); 3]. Elites and the enfranchised act against racist behavior in a society only when it serves them and their goals (Crenshaw, 1988; Hinrichs 2012; Taylor, 2015; Connerly 2007; Gillborn, 2009; Delgado and Stefancic 1995; Crenshaw et al., 1995); 4]. Race is a social construct. Modern genetics has confirmed this fact (Alfieri & Onwuachi-Willig, 2013; Mills, 1997; Delgado and Stefancic 1995; Crenshaw et al., 1995); 5]. Characteristics ascribed to a particular race will and do change. For example, Black people in the slavery era were most commonly called "happy-go-lucky and childlike," and unable to protect themselves, in order to rationalize slavery. Today, however, they are most commonly portrayed as "threatening and criminal," which rationalizes increased police intervention and lengthy prison terms (Huber & Solorzano, 2014; Delgado & Stefancic 1995; Crenshaw et al., 1995); and 6]. People have intersecting identities in that they belong to more than one demographic group and are consequently affected by disenfranchisement or inequality in more than one way. All individuals view the world through multiple lenses (Alfieri & Onwuachi-Willig, 2013; Connerly 2007; Mills, 1997; Subotnik, 1998; Delgado & Stefancic 1995; Crenshaw et al., 1995).

CRT validates its assertions by examining societal and institutional laws, regulations, policies, and their respective environments that support the status quo of White authority and Black subordination (Solorzano & Yosso, 2002; Taylor, 1999). The framework for CRT is predicated on historical ballot initiatives, court decisions and laws such as *Scott v. Sandford* (1856), the Dred Scott Decision (1857), the Naturalization Act (1790), the Washington State Affirmative Action Ban Initiative 200, and the 2014 U.S. Supreme Court ruling upholding a Michigan constitutional amendment banning affirmative action in admissions to the state's public universities (Cooper, 2002). The Justices concluded the 2015 term agreeing to revisit the use of race in admissions decisions by the University of Texas at Austin and hear *Fisher v. University of Texas*, No. 14-981 (Liptak, 2015). "The Court's 2013 decision in *Fisher v. University of Texas* reaffirmed that educational diversity is an interest sufficient to overcome the general ban on racial classifications by the government. But it added that public institutions must have good reasons for the methods they use to achieve that goal: A decision barring the use of race in admissions would undo a 2003 ruling that the majority said it expected to last for twenty-five years. In the 5-to-4 decision in *Grutter v. Bollinger,* the Supreme Court said that public colleges and universities could not use a point system to increase minority enrollment but could take race into account in vaguer ways to ensure academic diversity" (Liptak, 2015, p. A1.).

The use of affirmative action programs to overcome historic discrimination by public universities in their admissions policies was eliminated in California, Florida, Georgia, Texas, and Washington. Elimination of these programs occurred in three different forums: (1) in the courts, (2) in the voting booth, and (3) by executive order. Fearing drastic declines in minority enrollment on college campuses, higher education officials have been pursuing race-neutral alternatives for preserving diversity in the absence of affirmative action (Hinrichs, 2012; Kahlenberg, 2014). In particular, California, Florida, and Texas have each instituted percentage plans guaranteeing admission to undergraduate students who meet the state's class rank requirement. This work tells the story of the changing landscape of affirmative action in legal education in the quest to achieve student diversity and equity in SUS of Florida pre- and post-the OFI and its Talented Twenty Percent Plan (Marin, 2003; Shea, 2003).

## HISTORICAL FRAMEWORK AND CONTEXT

Affirmative action is one institutional practice in academia that non-White minorities can tell stories about that result in unintended benefits for the White majority (Dickinson, 2012; Aday, 2011; Solorzano & Yosso, 2002; Aguirre, 2000; Delgado, 1995; Crenshaw et al., 1995). One reason for telling this story is to illustrate how the elimination of affirmative action programs can be implemented in a manner that marginalizes minority law student recruitment/enrollment processes and results in benefits for majority persons (Aday, 2011; Aguirre, 2000; Crenshaw et al., 1995; Crenshaw, 2011; Delgado, 1995; Hinrichs 2012; Taylor, 2014). Another reason for telling the story is to sound an alarm, that for majority and minority stakeholders, diversity and equity programs replacing affirmative action programs can fall short of their goals if their implementation is simply treated as a bureaucratic activity in academia, and within the legal and public policy arenas (Aday, 2011; Aguirre, 2000; Connerly 2007). The U.S. Civil Rights Commission defines affirmative action as "any measure, beyond simple termination of a discriminatory practice, adopted to correct or compensate for past or present discrimination or to prevent discrimination from recurring in the future" (U.S. Commission on Civil Rights, 1977). According to The Leadership Conference on Civil Rights: "In practice, affirmative action takes positive steps to end discrimination, to prevent its recurrence, and to create new opportunities that were previously denied minorities and women" (The Leadership Conference, n.d.).

Prior to the Civil War, the 1800-1860 Black Codes restricted the civil rights and civil liberties of African Americans. Since becoming the 27th state in the United States on March 3, 1845, Florida, like other Southern states, has historically conducted systemic and structural higher education discrimination against African Americans. Enacted after the Reconstruction period of 1865–1877, Jim Crow laws (1877–1954) mandated de jure racial segregation in all public facilities in the former Confederate States of America, with a "separate but equal" status for African Americans.

Higher education segregation was promulgated at the national level as well. The 1862 Morrill Act signed into law by Abraham Lincoln established the Public Land-Grant System, to broaden access to higher education and drive economic development. The Morrill Act provided that "no state while in a condition of rebellion or insurrection against the government of the United States shall be entitled to the benefit of this act," in reference to the recent secession of several Southern states and the American Civil War that was raging at the time. The 2nd Morrill Act of 1890 established the Negro Public Land-Grant Institutions to accommodate the lack of access for Blacks to public higher education institutions in the Southern states.

The Florida Board of Control (1905–1965), established under the authority of the Buckman Act, sustained Florida's gender and racial segregation in its reorganization of the public higher education system as the SUS of Florida. The State Normal College for Colored Students, founded on October 3, 1887 and now known as Florida Agricultural and Mechanical University (FAMU), which is also an 1890 land grant institution, became an official member of the state system as a result of this change. It also paved the way for the Florida State College for Women founded in 1851 for Caucasian women only (and now known as Florida State University) and the University of the State of Florida founded in 1905 for Caucasian men only (and now known as University of Florida and an 1862 Public Land Grant Institution).

Segregationists were also pressured to reform in the 1940s with men and women veterans returning home from World War II. The GI Bill of Rights complicated things for the Florida Legislature, which also determined it necessary to make room for the World War II veterans wishing to pursue educational endeavors in the public higher education system leading to the elimination of gender but not racial segregation in 1947.

In an effort to maintain segregated schools, University of Florida (UF) College of Law in Gainesville, supported by the Florida Board of Control, denied admission to Virgil Darnell Hawkins and five other African American applicants solely on the basis of race. Hawkins and his allies prevailed before the U.S. Supreme Court in 1956, but not until twenty years later did Mr. Hawkins get a chance to practice law. Compelled by the denial of admission letter, dated May 13, 1949, Mr. Hawkins, a forty-one-year-old African American schoolteacher from Daytona Beach, FL, began a nine-year legal and political battle to gain admission to the only public law school in Florida at the time (Kathryn, 2014; Rivers, 2000).

> Before Virgil Hawkins took his stand there was no law school for African Americans in Florida. Rather than fund a separate institution in Florida or

> permit African Americans to attend an existing school with Whites, the State instituted a law in 1945 to provide scholarships for select African American students to study at segregated law schools outside the state. When Virgil Hawkins refused to accept that alternative, the Board of Control approved plans to open a segregated law school at Florida A&M College. By 1950, the U.S. Supreme Court had ruled on two related cases, *Sweatt v. Painter* and *McLaurin v. Oklahoma*. Despite these rulings, the Florida court still refused to admit Hawkins, and would continue to refuse even after the so-called Brown II decree issued by the Supreme Court in 1955 to clarify the original Brown decision. Hawkins persisted in his fight against the state's segregationist position, but more challenges were on the way. In 1958, the Board of Control established a new minimum score on the law school entry exam for incoming students, setting the admission threshold fifty points above Hawkins's 1956 score. As a result, Hawkins was officially denied not because of his race, but rather because he was disqualified by the new rules regarding test scores. Later that summer, federal district judge Dozier DeVane mandated that all qualified applicants be admitted to graduate and professional schools in Florida regardless of race. (Kathryn, 2014)

Hawkins's inaugural lawsuit against the Florida Board of Control charged that since UF's College of Law was the only tax-supported institution of its type in the state, "the denial of his application on the basis of race violated his civil rights under the equal protection of law clause of the Fourteenth Amendment to the U.S. Constitution" (Rivers, 2000, p. 16). However, the Florida Supreme Court, under the leadership of B.K. Roberts in his first term as Chief Justice (3/14/53–1/11/55), invoked the doctrine of states' rights to deny him admission, and the Justices agreed to allow Florida's alternative plan, which was to open a separate law school as promulgated by the Florida Board of Control on December 21, 1949. The Florida Agricultural and Mechanical College for Negroes College of Law (1949–1953), which later became the FAMU College of Law, admitted its first class in 1951 (Rivers, 2000; Legal Information Institute, n.d.). Its existence was short-lived. FAMU's last class entered in 1965 when the Florida Legislature defunded and closed the FAMU Law School and opened the Florida State University (FSU) College of Law within two miles of FAMU (Klink, 2003, p. 14). In his second term as Florida Supreme Court Chief Justice (7/1/61–7/1/65) B.K. Roberts succeeded in convincing Florida lawmakers that desegregation efforts such as the Civil Rights Act of 1964 eliminated the need for an all-Black law school. The Florida State University campus newspaper called on the citizens of Florida to thank Senator Pete Gibson, a Florida State alumnus who represented the 10th District (Madison and Taylor counties) "for the hard work he has done on this important piece of legislation" (The Florida Flambeau, 1965) that closed the Florida A&M University College established to uphold the separate but equal doctrine and opened the Florida State College of Law in defiance of the Civil Rights Act of 1964.

FSU honored Florida Supreme Court Chief Justice B.K. Roberts with the dedication of the B. K. Roberts Hall College of Law in 1971. But the story doesn't end there. On June 1, 1985, 17 years after legislative closing, political forces began a unified effort to reopen the FAMU College of Law (Rivers, 2000). By March of 2000, these efforts resulted in Florida Legislative Senate Bill 68, which created the Florida International University (FIU) College of Law and reversed the earlier 1965 legislative action that closed the FAMU College of Law. The OFI, contrary to its stated goal, served to leverage the creation of the Hispanic majority FIU College of Law and to reestablish the African American majority FAMU College of Law (Klink, 2003).

## SEPARATE AND UNEQUAL OUTCOMES

Unique to Hawkins's battle for justice and equal treatment under the law, Justice Joseph Hatchett, the first African American justice appointed and then elected to the Florida Supreme Court, compelled a 1976 unanimous decision to admit Hawkins to the Florida Bar and practice. Justice Hatchett's blistering 12-page dissent detailed "the injustice members of this Court once willfully wrought" with their "lawlessness on the part of men sworn to uphold the law" in their initial vote to deny the Florida Bar's request to allow Hawkins to practice in Florida. Even though the United States Supreme Court ruled in 1956 that he should be admitted to the school, the Florida Supreme Court invoked the doctrine of states' rights denying Hawkins admissions. By the time a federal district court judge ordered in 1958 that all University of Florida graduate schools be opened to all qualified African Americans, the Board of Control raised the entrance requirements, preventing Hawkins from enrollment (Associated Press, 1988).

One of those lawless men, B.K. Roberts, a 1928 graduate of UF Law School, was still there. The majority gave in to Hatchett, who diplomatically withdrew his dissent. In November 1976, the Florida Supreme Court, at the request of the Florida Bar, ruled 7-0 that Mr. Hawkins should be allowed to practice law and waived a requirement that he first take the bar exam. Soon after, Justice Roberts retired. President Jimmy Carter appointed Justice Hatchett to the 5th U.S. Circuit Court of Appeals on July 13, 1979 (St. Petersburg Times, 2004).

In 1977, after a 28-year battle to practice law in Florida that began by challenging the state's segregated higher-education system with an application to the all-White UF Law School in 1949, Mr. Hawkins opened his law practice in Leesburg, near his hometown of Okahumpka, Florida. But seven years later, at the age of seventy-seven, attorney Hawkins was before the Florida Supreme Court again because of allegations of improprieties in his legal practice. In January 1984, the Florida Supreme Court censured Mr. Hawkins and placed him on two years probation and he was allowed to resign from the Bar in April 1985 (Associated Press, 1988). Virgil Hawkins (See figure 2.1) determined and valiant soldier for justice and equal rights under the law is exemplary of the African American struggle in the Southern states and of the phrase "Justice too long delayed is justice denied" (King, 1963).

**Figure 2.1. Virgil Darnell Hawkins.**
Credit: State Archives of Florida, Florida Memory, http://floridamemory.com

Like many other African Americans, Mr. Hawkins was forced to pursue his legal training at the "separate but equal" Florida Agricultural and Mechanical College for Negroes (from 1949–1953) and University Law School (from 1954–1968) or leave the state. Hawkins graduated in 1964 from the unaccredited New England School of Law, in Boston Massachusetts. Justice Roberts was also instrumental in opening and closing the Florida A&M Law School in his respective first (3/14/53–1/11/55) and second (7/1/61–7/1/65) terms, affirmatively acting on behalf of White students and the White power structure. Florida A&M Law School was opened and closed to empower Whites and keep them from having to compete with Blacks. Virgil Hawkins fought and battled diligently for his and other Black people's constitutional rights to attend taxpayer supported universities and law schools of their choice in pursuit of their career goals and objectives, a right affirmatively afforded to their White counterparts such as Jonathan Kaney, J.D., the first student admitted to FSU College of Law in 1965 (See figure 2.2).

Prior to his admission, Kaney was the staffer to Senator Gibson whose bill respectively closed and opened FAMU and FSU Law Schools. Kaney was admitted to the Florida Bar and the U.S. Tax Court in 1969 a full ten years be-

**Figure 2.2. Jon Kaney, the first Florida State Law School student, was an administrative assistant in State Senator Pete Gibson's office during the 1965 session. He helped draft the bill establishing FSU's College of Law.**
Credit: Florida Department of State; https://www.floridamemory.com/items/show/25407

fore Virgil Hawkins was permitted in 1976 to practice law in Florida. Kaney graduated in 1969 with honors from the FSU College of Law and received the Master of Laws in 1979 from the UF College of Law. As of January 2015, Attorney Kaney was practicing as a business lawyer, counseling business corporations on tax, corporate and other areas of business law, handling mergers, acquisitions, business transactions, and dealing with estate planning for transfer of family businesses in the offices of Kaney & Olivari, P.L., Professional and Legal Help, Ormond Beach, FL (www.kaneyolivari.com).

## *Chapter Three*

# One Florida Initiative

## *The Race Neutral Policy in Florida*

Responding to challenges against the implications and effects of race preferences, the University of California Board of Regents in 1995 approved Ward Connerly's recommendation to eliminate all policies that granted "preferential treatment" (different standards) on the basis of race, sex, color, ethnicity or national origin. On November 6, 1996, the voters of California approved Proposition 209 commanding that all citizens be treated equally "without regard" to race and skin color (Ballotpedia, n.d.). The State of Washington followed in 1998 with Initiative 200, identical in language to Proposition 209. California and Washington, with the help of minority voters, served as models for subsequent initiatives in other states enacting "race neutral" legislation to improve minority representation in those states and to promote non-discrimination in government hiring and contracting. Hispanics, for example, turned out in higher numbers than any other group to support California's Proposition 209 (Milakovich & Gordon, 2001). They were followed by eight other states that sought to redress affirmative action through ballot initiatives.

Unlike other states, Florida voters did not have an opportunity to vote for or against affirmative action. Opposing a Florida ballot initiative attempt by Connerly et al., the State took a different tact when, on November 9, 1999, then Governor Jeb Bush and Lt. Governor Frank Brogan, signed Executive Order 99-281 implementing the One Florida Initiative (OFI; Connerly, 2007). The purpose of OFI was to increase opportunities and diversity in the SUS as well as in state contracting; however, the use of race was not permissible. "The OFI is diversity without quotas, preferences or set-asides. It was designated not to abandon affirmative action, but to substantively redefine it" (Bush, 2000). The OFI plan was also created to provide equity in education within the SUS by eliminating race and ethnicity as factors in admissions decisions (Bush, 2000). It was assumed that equity could be achieved by allowing the SUS to depend on other race neutral socioeconomic aspects in admissions decisions that can be related to race or ethnic factors, such as "income level, geography, special talents and whether an applicant is a first generation college student" (Bush, 2000). Bush believed that by employing these various dynamics, race neutral equity and diversity could be achieved.

Subsequently, state representative Tony Hill and state senator Kendrick Meeks launched a January 18–19, 2000 sit-in demonstration lasting for twenty-five hours in the office of Lt. Governor Frank Brogan. Bush ultimately agreed to meet with the two state legislators. His response was to propose a series of public hearings in Tampa, Miami, and Tallahassee to hear citizens' comments on the proposed initiative. Following the February hearings, which included strong opposition, Bush stated: "We are going forward with the OFI, we're going to push this through because we are working for the people and this is what the people want" (Paget-Clark, 1999).

Despite ongoing court challenges and vehement opposition from citizens, students, faculty members and community leaders, the Florida Board of Regents, under the leadership of Chancellor Adam Herbert, the first and only African American to lead the SUS of Florida (from 1998 to 2001), approved the OFI via the "Talented Twenty" rules with a 12–0 vote on February 17, 2000. The Talented Twenty set the new minimum SUS admissions standard for eligible high school students (Florida SUS Board of Governors Regulation BOG 6.002). "We've debated the [new admissions] rules and we're ready to move on," board chairman Tom Petway said after the vote. "Gov. Bush has a vision. What we're trying to do is what's best for our students" (Schuster, 2000, para.8). Chancellor Adam Herbert said, "This was a very significant day in the history of the State University System. We are going to, through this action, enhance diversity and open the doors of opportunity to some of the students in some of the poorest areas of our state" (Schuster, 2000, para.11). The following week the Florida Cabinet, meeting as the State Board of Education, approved the new admissions rules applying them to the year 2000 freshman class. The Board of Regents approved OFI with what was described as almost no plan, and very little guidance on how the program would be implemented in the state's public colleges and universities. A task force set up by the governor made recommendations to the Board of Regents, which would inform them how this policy would be implemented statewide.

Legislators Meeks and Hill were supported in their opposition when, on March 7, 2000, a statewide protest against the OFI drew an estimated 50,000 people to the State Capitol on the opening day of the Florida Legislature. Ultimately, Florida abandoned its use of long-accepted affirmative action practices with regard to contracting, hiring, and educational admission policies when it redefined affirmative action with implementation of the OFI by gubernatorial executive order. In fact, Governor Bush may have been correct in gauging the will of the majority of American citizens in saying, "It is what the people want" (Paget-Clarke, 1999). Governor Bush was also supported by his brother, President George W. Bush, who believed that "affirmative action is unconstitutional" (Bush, 2003). President Bush also stated that, "policies that give minorities a leg up on White applicants are unconstitutional discrimination and should be struck down by the Supreme Court" (Bush, 2003).

## IMPACT OF COURT CASES ON FLORIDA OFI

Affirmative action bans via ballot initiatives continue to be accompanied and affirmed by the judicial system (See tables 3.1–3.2). The 1st District Court of Appeals dismissed the Florida Conference of Branches of the National Association for the Advancement of Colored People's (NAACP) challenge to Governor Jeb Bush's One Florida Initiative on June 18, 2004 after a circuitous route that began in 1999 before an administrative law judge between the NAACP and the State. That judge upheld the 'Talented Twenty" OFI rules that eliminated racial and gender preferences in SUS of Florida admissions in 2000 and denied the State's claim that the NAACP did not have standing to bring the challenges. Both parties then appealed to the 1st District Court of Appeals, which reversed the administrative court finding against the State,

**Table 3.1. Statewide Affirmative Action Ban Ballot Initiatives**

| *Ballot Initiatives* | | *Year* | *Passed* | *Failed* |
|---|---|---|---|---|
| 1 | California Affirmative Action, Proposition 209 (1996) | 1996 | X | |
| 2 | Washington Affirmative Action Ban, Initiative 200 (1998) | 1998 | X | |
| 3 | Florida Civil Rights Initiative (2000) | 2000 | | X* |
| 4 | California Proposition 54, the "Racial Privacy Initiative" (October 2003) | 2003 | | X |
| 5 | Michigan Civil Rights Amendment, Proposal 2 (2006) | 2006 | X | |
| 6 | Colorado Discrimination and Preferential Treatment by Governments, Initiative 46 (2008) | 2008 | | X |
| 7 | Missouri Civil Rights Initiative (2008) | 2008 | | X |
| 8 | Nebraska Civil Rights Initiative, 424 (2008) | 2008 | X | |
| 9 | Arizona Civil Rights Amendment, Proposition 107 (2010) | 2010 | X | |
| 10 | Oklahoma Affirmative Action Ban Amendment, State Question 759 (2012) | 2012 | X | |

*Source:* http://ballotpedia.org/Affirmative_action_ballot_measures#tab=By_year
* Launched by Ward Connerly. Did not make the ballot.

**Table 3.2. Court Decisions on Affirmative Actions Bans**

| *Date* | *Decision* |
|---|---|
| 04/22/2014 | Supreme Court upheld Michigan affirmative action ban.[1] |
| 06/24/2013 | Supreme Court sent Texas affirmative action case back to lower court.[1] |
| 04/02/2012 | Ninth Circuit upheld California affirmative action ban.[1] |
| 08/02/2010 | California high court ruled affirmative action ban constitutional.[1] |
| xx/xx/2004 | Florida Court Upholds Executive Order Banning Affirmative Action.[2] |

*Source:* http://jurist.org/timelines/2014/06/state-bans-on-affirmative-action.php;[1] ………….[2]>

ruling that the NAACP did not have standing to bring the challenges. Having ruled, 4–3, upon appeal that the NAACP did have standing, the Florida Supreme Court sent the case back to the 1st District Court of Appeals in November 2003 (Associated Press, 2004).

It is indeed ironic that what was apparently working to achieve the kind of diversity that proponents were seeking has been dismantled. The very entity that brought about the changes, or made them possible, the nation's judicial system, has led to their downfall. Florida, like so many other states, was forced to seek new ways of achieving diversity in its higher education system based on litigation in other states and the likelihood of being the next state to be challenged in court by Ward Connerly via his previous affirmative action ballot and judicial accomplishments.

With regard to higher education, the OFI plan did not specifically address graduate and professional education within the SUS of Florida. The OFI, however, initiated the Talented Twenty Percent program for undergraduate education. The program substituted race and ethnic-based admissions guidelines by guaranteeing students admission to one of the 11 SUS of Florida institutions without regard to his or her American College Test or Scholastic Assessment Test scores, as long as the student graduated from a Florida public high school and was in the top 20 percent of their class. According to Bush (2000), the Talented Twenty program was expected to increase minority enrollment by approximately 1,200 students. Research shows that 410 minority students met the criteria by completing the college preparatory curriculum; however, there were 800 others who would be accepted if they completed their missing entrance credits prior to admission (Bush, 2000).

## FLORIDA CONFLATES OFI WITH PREDOMINANTLY BLACK AND HISPANIC LAW SCHOOLS

Some believe Governor Bush opposed and successfully countered Ward Connerly's anti-affirmative action ballot initiative with the OFI to help fend off negative perceptions of Black voters against his brother's run for President. The same can be said for the FAMU and FIU Law Schools. Bush countered the negative perceptions of Black voters about the OFI with the restoration of the FAMU College of Law, a majority Black institution. That and the new College of Law at FIU, a majority Hispanic institution, potentially helped to mitigate negative perceptions of Black voters against his brother, George W. Bush as well as repair his standing with the Hispanic and Black citizens of Florida, including those who voted 55–45 percent and 14 percent for him respectively in 1998 (Henderson, 2014).

During his tenure at FAMU as a faculty member (1964–1966; 1968–1974), and as the institution's eighth president, Frederick S. Humphries (1985–2001) witnessed "the College of Law being attacked from a number of fronts and then being phased out by the Legislature and Board of Regents" (Rivers, 2000). President Humphries spearheaded the effort to revive the law school after he decided that its return would be a major benefit to the institution, Florida, the legal profession, and the public, especially for members from groups underrepresented in law (Neyland, 2001). President Humphries knew that he would stand a better chance of success using the legislative route—convincing state lawmakers they should appropriate funds for the project. For example, FAMU General Counsel Bishop Clarke Holifield and Reginald J. Mitchell, executive assistant to President Humphries, developed 1990 and 1993 need statements supporting the fact that the law college "could provide a solution to the despairingly low numbers of Black law students, attorneys and judges in the state of Florida" (Rivers, 2000, p. 57). Holifield and Mitchell lobbied the Board of Regents, Florida and the National Bar Associations, FAMU National Alumni Association, and the Florida Legislature that the community needed the reestablishment of this institution (Neyland, 2000). Blacks within the Tallahassee community and across Florida began to get involved in petitioning for the re-establishment of the law school through various church endeavors (Neyland, 2000). The argument in favor of opening a new law school at FIU and reopening FAMU College of Law came down to one of educational necessity—the needs of the community for educated people in the workforce, the nation's courtrooms, and classrooms.

In 1991, Florida Senator Carrie P. Meek and Representative Alfred Lawson filed a bill to reestablish FAMU College of Law (Neyland, 2000). On March 20, 1991, Senator Meek's SB 1314 passed, directing "the Board of Regents to conduct a feasibility study for the possibility of establishing a new FAMU law school" (Rivers, 2000, p. 59). In addition, Chancellor Charles B. Reed and several of the Regents believed that minority representation in the legal profession could be enhanced by a multimillion-dollar pre-law and law scholarship program (Rivers, 2000). In 1994, the Florida Legislature established the Minority Participation in Legal Education (MPLE) Program, which aimed to address the underrepresentation of historically disadvantaged minorities practicing law in the State of Florida. Between 1994 and 2001, the Florida Education Fund sponsored annual scholarships for Florida residents enrolled in public and private law schools. A total of 533 scholars were supported from 1994 through 2005 via the Law Scholarship Program:

- 502 scholars (94 percent) graduated from law school and received their J.D. degrees.
- 94 percent of the graduates who took the Florida Bar examination passed.
- 95 percent of Program graduates who passed the Bar exam now practice law in Florida or practiced in the State for at least three years. (Florida Education Fund, n.d.)

Similarly, the Pre-Law Scholarship Program funded 305 students from 1994 through 2005. During this time:

- 239 scholars graduated and received their Bachelor's degrees.
- 134 graduates went on to attend Florida law schools, while 15 others enrolled in out-of-state schools.
- 56 of the remaining 90 graduates indicated that they would attend a Florida law school within two years of graduating from college as the program required. (Florida Education Fund, n.d.)

While studies by the Florida Post-Secondary Educational Planning Commission (PEPC), the Florida Board of Regents Legal Education Advisory Council (LEAC) and others, credited the MPLE program for increasing minority law school statewide,[1] the Florida Legislature voted to phase out the program in 2002.

In 1993, FIU was considered a site for a law school to help improve minority numbers in the legal profession (Neyland, 2000). This also generated a major push to reopen the school at FAMU. In 1994, Rev. R. B. Holmes of Tallahassee, and member-to-be of FAMU's first Board of Trustees in 2000, led a citywide march and spoke before the Board of Regents to plead for the law school (Thomas, 1994). According to Neyland (2000), State Representative Alfred Lawson filed six bills from 1991 through 1998 to propose the reestablishment of the FAMU law school. Others, however, would join the public outcry for reasons of their own. President Modesto Maidique had been lobbying the Florida legislature for one of Florida's public law schools since the mid-1980s. He saw the debate over OFI as his opportunity for success and met several times with the Board of Regents in an effort to establish the FIU College of Law.

A compromise was proposed in 2000, when State Senators Betty Holzendorf and Mario Diaz-Balart led a joint effort between Black and Hispanic legislators to create colleges of law at FAMU and FIU (Rivers, 2000). Proponents of a reopened FAMU law school and the opening of one at FIU for the Hispanic community saw their opportunity with debate in the legislature about the impact on minorities from Governor Bush's OFI. During the 2000 legislative session, Senate Bill 68 and House Bill 2129 were both filed. The FAMU College of Law (2001 Florida Statutes Chapter 240.7105) and FIU College of Law (2001 Florida Statutes Chapter 240.7101) were approved as a committee substitute for Senate Bill 68 (CS/SB 68) and signed into law on June 14, 2000 by Governor Jeb Bush as Chapter 2000-259. The rationale for adding these two MSI law schools to the state's other public schools of law was that they, along with the Governor's OFI, would provide additional access for minorities to enter the legal profession in Florida.

Adam Herbert, who was then Chancellor of the SUS of Florida, announced that the minority population in the SUS of Florida schools rose by 12 percent (Bush, 2000). Enrollment figures compiled by the SUS of Florida Chancellor's Office indicated that an additional 1,234 minorities (African American, Hispanic, Asian, and Native Americans) gained entry into the SUS of Florida (Bush, 2000). Governor Bush claimed that it had been proven that the State of Florida "can promote both opportunity and diversity in higher education without using unfair and legally suspect racial preferences" (Bush, 2000, p. 3). According to Bush, the data showed that, "while system-wide enrollment grew by approximately 11 percent, the number of African Americans at Florida State University grew by 21 percent and the number of African Americans at the University of Florida grew by 33 percent" (Bush, 2000, p. 3). The Hispanic population also increased at "the University of Florida by 19 percent and Florida State by 24 percent" (Bush, 2000, p. 3).

Governor Bush boasted that critics believed that the OFI would decrease the number of minorities at the flagship universities; however, that was not immediately evident based on information from the governor's office. According to Bush, "Minority enrollment actually flowed upwards toward the flagship universities" (Bush, 2000, p. 4). The SUS of Florida used various recruitment approaches, including intense recruitment of top performing students from low performing schools, to raise the level of minorities enrolled; however, race and ethnicity were not among the factors used by admissions personnel.

More recent data told a much different story. In reality, the consequence of the OFI has been a decrease in minority representation at most universities within the SUS of Florida. A 2006 article in the *Journal of Blacks in Higher Education* noted that since OFI's inception, the percentage of Blacks in the student body at six of the 11 campuses in the SUS declined ("Black Percentage," 2006). Further, in another 2006 article entitled "Raise Black Enrollment by Dropping One Florida" (2006), the editorial board of the Palm Beach Post discovered that enrollment of Blacks declined after OFI was implemented.

In addition to data questioning whether the OFI has helped to improve diversity in the SUS of Florida, there is evidence that suggests affirmative action does work. For example, medical students at University of California Davis School of Medicine who were admitted with lower grades and test scores as a result of affirmative action during a twenty-year period from 1968 to 1987 performed as well as other students in the program, according to research published in the October 1997 *Journal of the American Medical Association.* The study concluded: "An admissions process that allows for ethnicity and other special characteristics to be used heavily in admission decisions yields powerful effects on the diversity of the student population and shows no evidence of diluting the quality of the graduates" (Davidson & Lewis, 1997, p. 1154).

As a result of the OFI, which banned the use of race in admission decisions for undergraduate and graduate programs, Black enrollment decreased overall at the state's two most prominent law schools post-OFI in 2000. At UF, Black enrollment increased in 2000 and 2001 and then proceeded to decline through 2013. At FSU College of Law, Black enrollment decreased post-OFI from 2000 to 2013 compared to 1999 (See table 3.6). Black first year law enrollment diminished notably at the UF College of Law, down from 53 new students in 2000 to just 22 in 2004 (JBHE, 2006). Enrollment of Black first year students in 2005 was approximately 35; nearly 34 percent below the level that existed prior to the OFI. FSU College of Law also experienced a decline in Black enrollment. Its law school enrolled 23 Black students in the entering class of 2000; however, in 2005, only ten Black law students were enrolled in the first-year class (JBHE, 2006). Compiled from the SUS of Florida Board of Governors, the information in Tables 3.3 and 3.4 reports student enrollment by race and institution within Florida's public law schools, pre and post OFI, from 1998 to 2014.

According to the U.S. Census Bureau data, minorities were the fastest growing populations in states like Florida, California, and Texas during the last decade. It is a trend that is projected to continue, but at an even faster pace over the next two to three decades. Florida surpassed New York as the third most populace state in the year 2014 (U.S. Census, 2014), with Hispanic and Black populations responsible for most of the increases.

**Table 3.3. Total Florida State University System Enrollment by Race 1998–2013**

| | *1998* | *1999* | *2000* | *2001* | *2002* | *2003* | *2004* | *2005* | *2006* | *2007* | *2008* | *2009* | *2010* | *2011* | *2012* | *2013* | *Total* |
|---|---|---|---|---|---|---|---|---|---|---|---|---|---|---|---|---|---|
| Asian | 9,212 | 9,674 | 10,350 | 11,153 | 11,813 | 12,318 | 12,435 | 13,103 | 13,777 | 14,526 | 14,990 | 16,043 | 15,451 | | 14,883 | 14,745 | 29,628 |
| Black | 31,413 | 33,002 | 34,654 | 36,510 | 37,903 | 39,581 | 39,898 | 40,323 | 40,743 | 41,064 | 41,190 | 42,719 | 44,717 | 45,069 | 44,904 | 43,988 | 637,678 |
| Hispanic | 30,792 | 32,769 | 33,703 | 35,866 | 38,230 | 40,514 | 42,909 | 46,516 | 49,751 | 52,177 | 54,452 | 57,870 | 63,821 | 70,368 | 75,008 | 79,931 | 804,677 |
| Native American | 795 | 820 | 961 | 1,093 | 1,115 | 1,135 | 1,072 | 1,017 | 1,131 | 1,218 | 1,338 | 1,518 | 1,253 | 984 | 865 | 798 | 17,113 |
| Non Res. Alien | 8,506 | 9,635 | 10,351 | 11,062 | 11,576 | 10,917 | 12,401 | 12,427 | 11,179 | 12,006 | 12,282 | 12,944 | 13,089 | 13,784 | 14,545 | 15,579 | 192,283 |
| White | 142,231 | 145,382 | 147,967 | 152,966 | 157,432 | 162,136 | 164,192 | 168,726 | 172,251 | 174,876 | 173,003 | 175,352 | 174,454 | 172,879 | 171,312 | 167,898 | 2,623,057 |
| Pacific Islander | 0 | 0 | 0 | 0 | 0 | 0 | 0 | 0 | 0 | 0 | 0 | 0 | 291 | 472 | 638 | 786 | 2187 |
| Multiple | 0 | 0 | 0 | 0 | 0 | 0 | 0 | 0 | 0 | 0 | 0 | 0 | 2,959 | 5,581 | 7,078 | 8,118 | 23,736 |
| Not Reported | 973 | 1,417 | 2,767 | 3,334 | 4,284 | 4,736 | 4,655 | 5,223 | 5,184 | 5,268 | 5,258 | 5,813 | 5,468 | 5,625 | 5,756 | 5,907 | 71,668 |
| **Total** | **225,920** | **234,698** | **242,753** | **253,985** | **264,355** | **273,340** | **279,566** | **289,340** | **296,022** | **303,142** | **304,521** | **314,268** | **323,513** | **314,762** | **337,001** | **339,763** | **4,402,027** |

**Table 3.4. Florida Legal Professions and Studies Enrollment Data by University from 1998 to 2013***

| | *1998* | *1999* | *2000* | *2001* | *2002* | *2003* | *2004* | *2005* | *2006* | *2007* | *2008* | *2009* | *2010* | *2011* | *2012* | *2013* | *Grand Total* |
|---|---|---|---|---|---|---|---|---|---|---|---|---|---|---|---|---|---|
| FAMU | 0 | 0 | 0 | 0 | 89 | 194 | 291 | 394 | 531 | 558 | 603 | 607 | 671 | 714 | 662 | 518 | 5832 |
| FAU | 0 | 0 | 0 | 0 | 0 | 0 | 0 | 0 | 0 | 0 | 0 | 0 | 0 | 0 | 0 | 0 | 0 |
| FGCU | 0 | 0 | 0 | 0 | 0 | 0 | 0 | 0 | 0 | 0 | 0 | 0 | 0 | 0 | 0 | 0 | 0 |
| FIU | 0 | 0 | 0 | 0 | 102 | 196 | 284 | 331 | 384 | 452 | 533 | 620 | 587 | 551 | 511 | 496 | 5047 |
| FSU | 655 | 684 | 721 | 697 | 750 | 734 | 737 | 763 | 758 | 767 | 762 | 768 | 782 | 733 | 703 | 711 | 11725 |
| NCF | 0 | 0 | 0 | 0 | 0 | 0 | 0 | 0 | 0 | 0 | 0 | 0 | 0 | 0 | 0 | 0 | 0 |
| UCF | 0 | 0 | 0 | 0 | 0 | 0 | 0 | 0 | 0 | 0 | 0 | 0 | 0 | 0 | 0 | 0 | 0 |
| UF | 1,256 | 1,219 | 1,247 | 1,284 | 1,295 | 1,251 | 1,258 | 1,313 | 1,463 | 1,406 | 1,321 | 1,258 | 1,175 | 1,105 | 1,091 | 1,057 | 19,999 |
| UNF | 0 | 0 | 0 | 0 | 0 | 0 | 0 | 0 | 0 | 0 | 0 | 0 | 0 | 0 | 0 | 0 | 0 |
| USF | 0 | 0 | 0 | 0 | 0 | 0 | 0 | 0 | 0 | 0 | 0 | 0 | 0 | 0 | 0 | 0 | 0 |
| UWF | 0 | 0 | 0 | 0 | 0 | 0 | 0 | 0 | 0 | 0 | 0 | 0 | 0 | 0 | 0 | 0 | 0 |

**Source:* State University System of Florida Board of Governors, Interactive University Data

One gauge for how well Florida is producing a diverse legal profession equivalent to its population is enrollment data in the state's public law schools (See tables 3.3–3.4). Such observation revealed that in 2013, Blacks (434) were about 17 percent fewer in number than Hispanics (523) and both were lagging behind Whites (1,548) in law school enrollment (See table 3.4). The number of Black law students in Florida's four public law schools trended down in every school except the predominantly Black FAMU and predominantly Hispanic FIU through 2012, while the number of Hispanic law school students generally increased across the board. Post-OFI (2000 to 2013), Whites enjoyed the largest grand total increase in Florida law school enrollment, followed by Hispanics, Blacks, Asians, and finally Native Americans (See table 3.4). According to the Florida Bar Association (FBA) Diversity in the Legal Profession 2009 Status Report, the racial demographics for members in good standing (active and inactive) of the Florida Bar was 9 percent Hispanic, 3 percent African American, and 1 percent Asian/ Pacific Islander. Compiled from the SUS of Florida Board of Governors, the information in tables 3.5 through 3.8 reports student enrollment by race and institution at each of Florida's four public law schools, pre and post OFI, from 1998 to 2013.

## NATIONAL DATA ON LEGAL EDUCATION AND PRACTICE

Nationally, the percentage of minorities enrolled in law schools increased during the 2009, 2010, and 2011 academic years at 22.4 percent, 23.8 percent, and 24.5 percent respectively (American Bar Association, 2012). According to ABA Commission on Racial and Ethnic Diversity, the 2010 Census reported that people of color comprised 36.3 percent of the United States population (See table 3.9). At the beginning of the 2011 bar year, the ABA's total membership was 337,453; 114,396 of the members reported their race, ethnicity, or gender. In contrast to the U.S. population, minorities constituted less than 10 percent of the Association's membership according to reported figures (See table 3.10).

The "Miles to Go: Progress of Minorities in the Legal Profession" study conducted by the ABA's Commission on Racial and Ethnic Diversity found that the representation of African Americans in the legal profession is lower than their representation in other fields (2005). Chambliss (2004) described the reduction of minority enrollment in the profession as extremely troubling. "In 2000, African Americans made up only 3.9 percent of all lawyers, compared to 4.4 percent of all physicians, 5.6 percent of college and university professors, 7.8 percent of computer scientists, and 7.0 percent of accountants

**Table 3.5. University of Florida Legal Professions and Studies Enrollment Data by Race from 1998 to 2013***

| | *1998* | *1999* | *2000* | *2001* | *2002* | *2003* | *2004* | *2005* | *2006* | *2007* | *2008* | *2009* | *2010* | *2011* | *2012* | *2013* | *Total* |
|---|---|---|---|---|---|---|---|---|---|---|---|---|---|---|---|---|---|
| Asian | 54 | 50 | 47 | 46 | 45 | 47 | 65 | 62 | 71 | 70 | 76 | 77 | 63 | 48 | 40 | 36 | 897 |
| Black | 109 | 111 | 134 | 148 | 121 | 99 | 80 | 86 | 85 | 82 | 69 | 71 | 69 | 66 | 46 | 67 | 1443 |
| Hispanic | 119 | 144 | 148 | 165 | 145 | 123 | 112 | 123 | 134 | 127 | 124 | 114 | 120 | 117 | 136 | 141 | 2092 |
| Native American | 5 | 9 | 9 | 10 | 8 | 8 | 5 | 3 | 4 | 7 | 6 | 12 | 6 | 7 | 12 | 11 | 122 |
| Non Res. Alien | 4 | 20 | 18 | 22 | 30 | 26 | 24 | 30 | 43 | 30 | 43 | 62 | 36 | 43 | 32 | 31 | 494 |
| White | 902 | 886 | 884 | 917 | 891 | 812 | 907 | 950 | 1,081 | 1,048 | 954 | 860 | 804 | 748 | 740 | 691 | 14,075 |
| Pacific Islander | 0 | 0 | 0 | 0 | 0 | 0 | 0 | 0 | 0 | 0 | 0 | 0 | 0 | 0 | 1 | 1 | 2 |
| Multiple | 0 | 0 | 0 | 0 | 0 | 0 | 0 | 0 | 0 | 0 | 0 | 0 | 14 | 17 | 15 | 13 | 59 |
| Not Reported | | 1 | 5 | 9 | 29 | 57 | 65 | 59 | 45 | 42 | 49 | 62 | 63 | 59 | 69 | 66 | 680 |
| **Total** | **1,183** | **1,219** | **1,247** | **1,284** | **1,295** | **1,251** | **1,258** | **1,313** | **1,463** | **1,406** | **1,321** | **1,258** | **1,175** | **1,105** | **1,091** | **1,057** | **19,864** |

**Source:* State University System of Florida Board of Governors, Interactive University Data

**Table 3.6. Florida State University Legal Professions and Studies Enrollment Data by Race from 1998 to 2003**

| | *1998* | *1999* | *2000* | *2001* | *2002* | *2003* | *2004* | *2005* | *2006* | *2007* | *2008* | *2009* | *2010* | *2011* | *2012* | *2013* | *Total* |
|---|---|---|---|---|---|---|---|---|---|---|---|---|---|---|---|---|---|
| Asian | 10 | 12 | 18 | 21 | 19 | 25 | 33 | 36 | 35 | 27 | 19 | 17 | 23 | 25 | 16 | 19 | 355 |
| Black | 79 | 70 | 66 | 63 | 64 | 57 | 50 | 42 | 46 | 45 | 50 | 58 | 54 | 54 | 56 | 60 | 914 |
| Hispanic | 64 | 56 | 62 | 64 | 76 | 69 | 66 | 64 | 62 | 56 | 47 | 50 | 71 | 73 | 67 | 64 | 1011 |
| Native American | 7 | 7 | 3 | 4 | 5 | 5 | 7 | 7 | 5 | 4 | 4 | 3 | 2 | 1 | 3 | 11 | 78 |
| Non Res. Alien | 2 | 2 | 4 | 2 | 2 | 1 | 1 | 2 | 4 | 6 | 10 | 8 | 4 | 5 | 11 | 10 | 74 |
| White | 493 | 537 | 568 | 543 | 567 | 561 | 565 | 592 | 582 | 597 | 575 | 574 | 577 | 540 | 510 | 511 | 8892 |
| Pacific Islander | 0 | 0 | 0 | 0 | 0 | 0 | 0 | 0 | 0 | 0 | 0 | 0 | 0 | 0 | 0 | 1 | 1 |
| Multiple | 0 | 0 | 0 | 0 | 0 | 0 | 0 | 0 | 0 | 0 | 0 | 0 | 14 | 17 | 15 | 13 | 59 |
| Not Reported | 0 | 0 | 0 | 0 | 17 | 16 | 15 | 20 | 24 | 32 | 57 | 58 | 51 | 34 | 37 | 34 | 395 |
| **Total** | **655** | **684** | **721** | **697** | **750** | **734** | **737** | **763** | **758** | **767** | **762** | **768** | **782** | **733** | **703** | **711** | **11779** |

**Source*: State University System of Florida Board of Governors, Interactive University Data

**Table 3.7. Florida International University Legal Professions and Studies Enrollment Data by Race 1998 to 2013**

| | *1998* | *1999* | *2000* | *2001* | *2002* | *2003* | *2004* | *2005* | *2006* | *2007* | *2008* | *2009* | *2010* | *2011* | *2012* | *2013* | *Total* |
|---|---|---|---|---|---|---|---|---|---|---|---|---|---|---|---|---|---|
| Asian | 0 | 0 | 0 | 0 | 1 | 3 | 8 | 8 | 8 | 10 | 11 | 15 | 21 | 16 | 13 | 10 | 124 |
| Black | 0 | 0 | 0 | 0 | 8 | 19 | 32 | 35 | 38 | 38 | 46 | 53 | 54 | 58 | 58 | 42 | 481 |
| Hispanic | 0 | 0 | 0 | 0 | 45 | 82 | 120 | 135 | 170 | 193 | 237 | 274 | 249 | 229 | 228 | 230 | 2192 |
| Native American | 0 | 0 | 0 | 0 | 0 | 1 | 1 | 2 | 2 | 1 | 0 | 4 | 4 | 4 | 6 | 4 | 29 |
| Non Res. Alien | 0 | 0 | 0 | 0 | 1 | 0 | 3 | 3 | 1 | 5 | 4 | 4 | 2 | 4 | 5 | 4 | 36 |
| White | 0 | 0 | 0 | 0 | 45 | 82 | 113 | 140 | 153 | 185 | 214 | 253 | 243 | 233 | 197 | 202 | 2060 |
| Pacific Islander | 0 | 0 | 0 | 0 | 0 | 0 | 0 | 0 | 0 | 0 | 0 | 0 | 0 | 0 | 0 | 0 | 0 |
| Multiple | 0 | 0 | 0 | 0 | 0 | 0 | 0 | 0 | 0 | 0 | 0 | 0 | 4 | 3 | 1 | 1 | 9 |
| Not Reported | 0 | 0 | 0 | 0 | 2 | 9 | 7 | 8 | 12 | 20 | 21 | 17 | 10 | 4 | 3 | 3 | 116 |
| **Total** | **0** | **0** | **0** | **0** | **750** | **734** | **284** | **331** | **384** | **452** | **533** | **620** | **587** | **551** | **511** | **496** | **5047** |

**Source:* State University System of Florida Board of Governors, Interactive University Data

**Table 3.8. Florida A&M University Legal Professions and Studies Enrollment Data by Race from 1998 to 2013**

| | *1998* | *1999* | *2000* | *2001* | *2002* | *2003* | *2004* | *2005* | *2006* | *2007* | *2008* | *2009* | *2010* | *2011* | *2012* | *2013* | *Total* |
|---|---|---|---|---|---|---|---|---|---|---|---|---|---|---|---|---|---|
| Asian | 0 | 0 | 0 | 0 | 1 | 3 | 8 | 11 | 18 | 18 | 20 | 22 | 26 | 25 | 20 | 15 | **187** |
| Black | 0 | 0 | 0 | 0 | 8 | 19 | 113 | 172 | 269 | 281 | 297 | 273 | 336 | 397 | 348 | 265 | **2778** |
| Hispanic | 0 | 0 | 0 | 0 | 45 | 82 | 32 | 53 | 82 | 81 | 96 | 98 | 68 | 82 | 90 | 88 | **897** |
| Native American | 0 | 0 | 0 | 0 | 0 | 1 | 2 | 4 | 4 | 5 | 7 | 5 | 4 | 5 | 5 | 5 | **47** |
| Non Res. Alien | 0 | 0 | 0 | 0 | 1 | 0 | 1 | 0 | 0 | 0 | 0 | 0 | 1 | 0 | 0 | 0 | **3** |
| White | 0 | 0 | 0 | 0 | 45 | 82 | 135 | 153 | 157 | 150 | 168 | 209 | 234 | 204 | 198 | 144 | **1879** |
| Pacific Islander | 0 | 0 | 0 | 0 | 0 | 0 | 0 | 0 | 0 | 0 | 0 | 0 | 0 | 0 | 0 | 0 | **0** |
| Multiple | 0 | 0 | 0 | 0 | 0 | 0 | 0 | 0 | 0 | 0 | 0 | 0 | 2 | 1 | 1 | 1 | **5** |
| Not Reported | 0 | 0 | 0 | 0 | 2 | 9 | 0 | 1 | 1 | 23 | 15 | 0 | 0 | 0 | 0 | 0 | **51** |
| **Total** | **655** | **684** | **721** | **697** | **750** | **734** | **291** | **394** | **531** | **558** | **603** | **607** | **671** | **714** | **662** | **518** | **5847** |

**Source:* State University System of Florida Board of Governors, Interactive University Data

**Table 3.9. U.S. Census 2010 Minority Demographics**

| *Race/Ethnicity* | *Percent of General Population* |
|---|---|
| African American | 12.2 percent |
| Hispanic | 4.9 percent |
| African American | 16.39 percent |
| Native American | 0.7 percent |

and auditors" (Mallory, 2005, p. 5). Data provided by the ABA confirms that while Blacks represent 16 percent of the population in the United States, they only make up approximately 4 percent of the nation's lawyers (See tables 3.9 and 3.10). This lack of representation has far ranging effects in the distrust of the legal system by racial minorities, due to the lack of lawyers and judges who share similar identities (Randall, 2004). Kim Keenan, NAACP General Counsel and Past President (2004) of the National Bar Association (NBA), indicated then that as a result of the underrepresentation of African Americans in the legal profession, individuals, communities, organizations and businesses will find it difficult to find lawyers of color to represent and adjudicate them on legal and public policy issues, especially those issues disproportionately affecting people of color (Mallory, 2005).

If the statement is true, that 'justice is blind,' then it should be clear to all that this does not apply to America's public and private law schools. They are still very much the bastions of a White dominated world (See table 3.11). Unlike so many other professions, it appears that the legal profession is able to maintain the look it has had for the past several decades. It is a defiant look of non-diversity, resisting efforts to make substantive changes.

**Table 3.10. ABA Membership Total Per Year**

| | *Actual Figures/Percentages* | | | | | |
|---|---|---|---|---|---|---|
| | *2000–2001* | | *2010–2011* | | *2011–2012* | |
| *Race/Ethnicity* | # | % | # | % | # | % |
| African American | 3,777 | 2.71 | 4,156 | 3.49 | 4,042 | 3.53 |
| Asian American | 3,483 | 2.50 | 3,670 | 3.08 | 3,460 | 3.02 |
| Hispanic | 3,165 | 2.27 | 3,282 | 2.75 | 3,167 | 2.77 |
| Native American | 828 | 0.59 | 677 | 0.57 | 646 | 0.56 |
| Caucasian | 126,480 | 90.88 | 105,470 | 88.54 | 101,262 | 88.52 |
| Other | 1,439 | 1.03 | 1,861 | 1.56 | 1,819 | 1.59 |
| Unknown | 269,513 | 0 | 208,427 | 0 | 223,057 | 0 |
| Total | 408,685 | 100 | 327,543 | 100 | 337,453 | 100 |

**Table 3.11. ABA Approved Law School Faculty & Staff Members Ethnicity and Gender: Fall 2013**

| | *FEMALE* | | | *MALE* | | |
|---|---|---|---|---|---|---|
| | *Total Minorities** | *Caucasian* | *Total** | *Total Minorities* | *Caucasian* | *Total*** |
| **Full Time Teaching Resources** | | | | | | |
| Tenured | 399–22.6% | 1,353–76.7% | 1,766–16.3% | 508–14.0% | 3,096–85.2% | 3,632–27.0% |
| Tenure-Track | 252–34.5% | 464–63.5% | 731–6.7% | 208–26.7% | 546–70.2% | 778–5.8% |
| 405c | 154–14.7% | 880–84.1% | 1,046–9.7% | 86–13.8% | 530–85.1% | 623–4.6% |
| Visitors | 24–20.5% | 81–69.2% | 117–1.1% | 21–13.5% | 119–76.3% | 156–1.2% |
| All Full Time | 829–22.7% | 2,778–75.9% | 3,659–33.8% | 823–15.9% | 4291–82.7% | 5,189–38.5% |
| **Other Teaching Resources** | | | | | | |
| Full Time Skills | 43–26.7% | 115–71.4% | 161–1.5% | 12–13.0% | 76–82.6% | 92–0.7% |
| Full Time Writing | 14–8.4% | 146–87.4% | 167–1.5% | 9–14.8% | 42–68.9% | 61–0.5% |
| Other Full Time | 89–18.0% | 391–79.1% | 494–4.6% | 34–9.3% | 314–85.6% | 367–2.7% |
| Part Time | 378–14.0% | 2,179–80.9% | 2,694–24.9% | 505–86.1% | 4,882–86.1% | 5,667–42.1% |
| **Administrators** | | | | | | |
| Dean | 17–29.3% | 41–70.7% | 58–0.5% | 25–17.4% | 119–82.6% | 144–1.1% |
| Associate or Vice Dean | 89–24.4% | 274–75.1% | 365–3.4% | 70–20.3% | 273–79.4% | 344–2.6% |
| Assistant Dean/ Director | 542–25.2% | 1,590–73.9% | 2,152–19.9% | 225–21.9% | 785–76.3% | 1,029–7.6% |
| **Full Time Professional Librarians** | 207–19.1% | 866–79.7% | 1,086–10.0% | 88–15.1% | 480–84.2% | 582–4.3% |
| **Total** | 2,208–20.4% | 8,380–77.3% | 10,836–100% | 1,791–13.3% | 11,272 –83.7% | 13,475–100% |

In graduate and professional programs, statistics suggest that predominantly White institutions would do well to recruit more minority students (Jones, 2005). The largest group of minorities and therefore largest pool of potential students in the United States is Hispanics followed by African Americans (U.S. Census Bureau, 2014). These two ethnic minorities, however, are largely underrepresented in many specialized fields, such as the legal profession. Barker (2005) indicated that Blacks and Hispanics accounted for slightly more than 5 percent of lawyers in the top 250 grossing law firms in the country. Minorities are significantly underrepresented in the legal profession. For example, the Florida Bar (2004) reported that there are 74,125 members of the Florida Bar, of whom 43,007 reported their race, and of that number, minorities made up less than 10 percent. Additionally, of the 2,056 members on standing committees of the Florida Bar, minorities comprise slightly more than 20 percent, including: 13 percent Hispanic, 6 percent African American, 1 percent Asian/Pacific Islander, and less than 1 percent that are of another minority group (The Florida Bar, 2006). in 2000, 88.8 percent of lawyers were White. In 2010, this percentage only slightly dropped .07 percent with 88.1 percent of lawyers being White (ABA, 2015).

In 2005, fewer individuals applied to law schools, therefore minority enrollment also dropped (Jones, 2005). The enrollment of women in law schools increased in 2005, with the University of California Los Angeles (UCLA) reporting the highest percentage of women enrolled in law programs at 50 percent. As a result of fewer applicants, ethnic diversity within U.S. law schools will suffer. "The law school with the highest percentage of minority enrollment for this year (2005) was University of Pennsylvania, with 38 percent of its incoming class indicating minority status" (Jones, 2005, p. 3).

The ABA (2006) found that the total minority enrollment in Doctor of Jurisprudence programs has indeed increased between 1971 and 1992. During the period 1971 to 1992, the total minority enrollment of all law school students was 5,568 (ABA, 2006). The number of minority law school students expanded in 2005–2006 to 29,768 total enrollments (ABA, 2006). However, while the absolute number increased, the *Journal of Blacks in Higher Education* (2007) found that the percentage of Blacks enrolled in all law schools declined from 7 percent in 1997 to 6 percent in 2007. "The majority of the nation's 30 highest-ranked law schools have shown a decline in Black enrollment" ("Declining Black Enrollment," 2007). In his suggestion that law schools are using diversity as a means of survival, Taylor (2015) notes that nearly ten years later, law school student bodies are becoming more diverse than ever, with students of color accounting for 26 percent of enrollment, however, this is only in an effort to combat the drop in White student enrollment.

## RESEARCH ON TOP SCHOOLS ENROLLING MINORITIES

According to Smith-Barrow (2016), St. Mary's University in Texas, University of the District of Columbia in Washington, DC, Western State College of Law at Argosy University in California, Southern University Law Center in Baton Rouge, Louisiana, Florida International University in Miami, Florida, North Carolina Central University in Durham, North Carolina, Richardson School of Law at University of Hawaii-Manoa, St. Thomas University, Texas Southern University, and Howard University are among the top ten law schools with over 52 percent minority enrollment. As a general rule, those colleges and universities that enroll the largest number of minority graduate students are situated in areas with the largest population of minorities. This can be observed with the list of law schools with high minority enrollment. As an example, the National Science Foundation collected data on trends in Science and Engineering students, which shows that the schools with the highest number of Hispanic graduate students are located in states with large numbers of Hispanics—such as Puerto Rico, California, Texas, and Florida. Similarly, five of the institutions with high Asian graduate student enrollment are in California, while more than half of the top ten graduate schools with the largest enrollment numbers for African American students are HBCUs. All of the states with high minority enrollment, with the exception of two, are based in Southern states (NSF, 1997).

More current and complete data for graduate schools with the largest enrollment of minority students and number of minority graduates, that is, data beyond 1997, is woefully lacking today. There has been little research done that yields up-to-date information on enrollment trends by ethnicity, broken down by individual colleges and universities. In addition, the websites and annual reports that are done by the organizations such as Council of Graduate Studies, National Center for Education Statistics, Educational Testing Service, American Council on Education, and the Carnegie Foundation for Excellence in Teaching do not yield data in the aggregate. The most recent and useful data available today would appear to be that which is collected by such publications as *U.S. News & World Report, Diverse Issues of Higher Education*, and *Hispanic Business Magazine*. The information gleaned from the annual reports in these publications is the result of extensive surveys sent to each of the schools and from data collected by the U.S. Department of Education. Still, the data is organized not by institutions with the "largest minority populations," but by institutions described as "best schools for minority graduate students" and, in some cases, "colleges graduating the largest number of minorities" (U.S. News & World Report; Hispanic Business

Magazine). Nevertheless, it is perhaps the best information available on the subject and is the data presented in this study.

## NOTE

1. See the Interim Report of LEAC, March 9, 2000; MPLE Program Report and Recommendations by PEPC, December 1999; A review of the MPLE Program for the Florida Board of Regents by MGT of America, Inc., February 18, 1999; and An Update on the Capacity for Legal Education for the Florida Bar by the National Center for Higher Education Management Systems, Preliminary Draft, 1998.

# *Chapter Four*

# Methodology

The purpose of this study was to determine what, if any, impact the gubernatorial executive order eliminating affirmative action in Florida (OFI) and the simultaneous addition of predominantly Black and predominantly Hispanic law schools had on racial and ethnic diversity in the state's public law schools and its legal profession.

## RESEARCH QUESTIONS

Based on the purpose of the study, the following research questions (RQ) were addressed:

RQ 1: How has the implementation of OFI impacted the (a) mission statements, (b) recruitment efforts and (c) admission practices of Florida's public law schools?

RQ 2: How has the addition of minority serving institutions (MSIs; predominantly Black Florida A&M University and predominantly Hispanic Florida International University law schools) impacted the (a) mission statements, (b) recruitment efforts and (c) admission practices of Florida's public law schools?

RQ 3: How has the implementation of OFI impacted the (a) diversity of student applicants, (b) admissions, (c) enrollment, and (d) Law School Admission Test (LSAT) scores of Florida's public law schools?

RQ 4: How has the implementation of OFI impacted (a) the diversity of Florida's legal profession graduates and (b) those admitted to the Florida Bar?

RQ 5: How has the addition of minority serving institutions (MSIs; predominantly Black Florida A&M University and predominantly Hispanic Florida International University law schools) impacted the (a) diversity of student applicants, (b) admissions, (c) enrollment, and (d) LSAT scores of Florida's public law schools?

RQ 6: How has the addition of minority serving institutions (MSIs; predominantly Black Florida A&M University and predominantly Hispanic Florida International University law schools) impacted the (a) diversity of Florida's legal profession graduates and (b) those admitted to the Florida Bar?

## HYPOTHESES

Research questions 1 and 2 are qualitative in nature and therefore do not have hypotheses. Associated with quantitative research, questions 3, 4, 5 and 6, are null and alternative hypotheses grouped under the headings One Florida Initiative (See table 4.1) and Minority Serving Institutions (See table 4.2).

**Table 4.1. Data Analysis Schema**

| *Hypothesis* | *Independent Variable* | *Dependent Variable* | *Statistical Hypothesis* | *Statistical Procedure* |
|---|---|---|---|---|
| 1 | Before and After OFI | percentage of minority applicants | $p_1 = p_2$ <br> $p_1 \neq p_2$ | Z-test of Proportion |
| 2 | Before and After OFI | percentage of minorities admitted | $p_1 = p_2$ <br> $p_1 \neq p_2$ | Z-test of Proportion |
| 3 | Before and After OFI | percentage of minorities enrolled | $p_1 = p_2$ <br> $p_1 \neq p_2$ | Z-test of Proportion |
| 4 | Before and After OFI | LSAT Scores | $\mu_1 = \mu_2$ <br> $\mu_1 \neq \mu_2$ | ANOVA |
| 5 | Before and After OFI | percentage of minority graduates | $p_1 = p_2$ <br> $p_1 \neq p_2$ | Z-test of Proportion |
| 6 | Before and After OFI | percentage of minority law school graduates sitting for the FL Bar | $p_1 = p_2$ <br> $p_1 \neq p_2$ | Z-test of Proportion |
| 7 | Before and After MSI | percentage of minority applicants | $p_1 = p_2$ <br> $p_1 \neq p_2$ | Z-test of Proportion |
| 8 | Before and After MSI | percentage of minorities admitted | $p_1 = p_2$ <br> $p_1 \neq p_2$ | Z-test of Proportion |
| 9 | Before and After MSI | percentage of minorities enrolled | $p_1 = p_2$ <br> $p_1 \neq p_2$ | Z-test of Proportion |
| 10 | Before and After MSI | LSAT Scores | $\mu_1 = \mu_2$ <br> $\mu_1 \neq \mu_2$ | ANOVA |
| 11 | Before and After MSI | percentage of minority graduates | $p_1 = p_2$ <br> $p_1 \neq p_2$ | Z-test of Proportion |
| 12 | Before and After MSI | percentage of minority law school graduates sitting for the FL Bar | $p_1 = p_2$ <br> $p_1 \neq p_2$ | Z-test of Proportion |

## DESIGN OF THE STUDY

This study utilized in-depth structured interviews and questionnaires (Mingers & Brocklesby, 1997) in an effort to gain perceptions of administrators about the impacts of the OFI on Florida's law schools. A case study approach was employed to discern academic administrators' views about redefining the role of affirmative action in recruiting, admissions, and enrollment of SUS of Florida law schools. A case study involves the information related to a person or group of people by way of observing, interviewing, and using other evidence. It is similar in this regard to ethnographic research—offering a way to learn about a complicated circumstance by using descriptive and contextual analysis (Yin,1994). The study also utilized pre- and post-OFI application, admission, and enrollment data from the SUS of Florida Board of Governors to determine respective changes.

The target population of this study included law school deans and admissions personnel employed at the four public law schools in Florida: UF, FSU, FIU, and FAMU. These individuals were selected as participants because they could personally examine the growth of diversity after the initiative was implemented and following the dilution of conventional affirmative action policies in Florida. These individuals were also able to provide institutional knowledge as members of the staff. There was near unanimous participation in the study among those individuals contacted. Each of the law school deans and admissions personnel who agreed to take part in the research did so willingly, either by email or by in-person interview. The views of all but one of the four public law schools in Florida were represented in the study. Neither the dean nor the admissions personnel at FAMU College of Law agreed to participate in this study due to personnel changes at the school.

The in-depth structured interviews in this study consisted of open-ended questions conducted with law school deans and admissions personnel from three of the four public law schools in Florida. The questions were devised and tested in a pilot study with university administrators to determine whether the questions were sound and to approximate the time commitment necessary to participate in the study (Hamel, Dufour, and Fortin, 1993; Denzin and Lincoln, 1994; and Merriam 1998). A copy of the interview questions is included in the appendix (See appendix B).

Secondary data sets provided by the SUS of Florida Board of Governors (enrollment data from 1998–2006) and the Florida Bar Association (membership data from 1998–2006) were used to gather descriptive statistics and to analyze the null hypotheses. The enrollment data employed within the study was compiled by race or ethnic make-up and by institution. The annual data prior to the enactment of the OFI (1998–1999) was used as the base year for the study. Since the law was enacted in November 1999, the first real post year of implementation was the 2000–2001 academic year, which was analyzed and used to determine whether there were differences in the variables of interest compared to 1998–1999 and in any of the subsequent years. The statistics used to compare the before and after-effects of the implementation of the OFI and the MSI Law Schools included percentage change in minority applications, admissions, enrollments, graduates, and graduates sitting for the Florida Bar; and the differences between the mean law school admission test scores (See table 4.2).

This study also relied on document and artifact analyses of reports, transcripts, newspaper articles, legislation, legislation analysis, the OFI Executive Order, and other official records from the Florida Education Fund and the Postsecondary Education Planning Commission. Primary research from the Board of Regents, SUS of Florida Board of Governors and the Florida Senate Committee on Education was also reviewed to discern the legal education and profession impacts of the OFI (Weston, 2005; West and Turner, 2004; Mer-

**Table 4.2. Minority Serving Institution Impacts on Florida Public Law Schools**

| | *Null Hypothesis Ho* | *Alternative Hypothesis Ha* |
|---|---|---|
| 5a | There is no significant difference in the percentage of minority **applicants** to the public law schools following the creation of MSI law schools. | There is a significant difference in the percentage of minority applicants to the public law schools following the creation of MSI law schools. |
| 5b | There is no significant difference in the percentage of minorities **admitted** to the public law schools following the creation of MSI law schools. | There is a significant difference in the percentage of minorities admitted to the public law schools following the creation of MSI law schools. |
| 5c | There is no significant difference in the percentage of minorities **enrolled** at the public law schools following the creation of MSI law schools. | There is a significant difference in the percentage of minorities enrolled at the public law schools following the creation of MSI law schools. |
| 5d | There is no significant difference in the average **LSAT scores** of the public law schools following the creation of MSI law schools. | There is a significant difference in the average LSAT scores of the public law schools following the creation of MSI law schools. |
| 6a | There is no significant difference in the percentage of minority **graduates** at the public law schools following the creation of MSI law schools. | There is a significant difference in the percentage of minority graduates at the public law schools following the creation of MSI law schools. |
| 6b | There is no significant difference in the percentage of minority law school graduates **admitted to the Florida Bar** following the creation of MSI law schools. | There is a significant difference in the percentage of minority law school graduates admitted to the Florida Bar following the creation of MSI law schools. |

riam, 1998; Yin, 1994; and Fisher, 1985). Institutional Review Board (IRB) approval from Morgan State University was granted in the fall of 2006, prior to the pilot study being conducted. Following the IRB approval, the SUS of Florida law schools' IRB committees were contacted with a letter indicating the particulars about the research being examined. IRB approval was requested and also granted by those institutions.

# *Chapter Five*

# Findings

The key question of this study was: "Have Florida's public law schools increased access, enrollment, and production of minority law students and professionals following implementation of the One Florida Initiative as an alternative to affirmative action and the simultaneous addition of two Minority Serving Institution's law schools?" The study proposed six primary research questions: 1 and 2 were qualitative in nature; 3, 4, 5, and 6 were quantitative and associated with twelve null and alternative hypotheses. Three of the four colleges of law agreed to participate in the study, while a fourth declined to respond. The findings for the study and the results of testing the hypotheses follow and are grouped under each of the research questions.

## IMPACT OF OFI ON LAW SCHOOL MISSION STATEMENTS

Research question 1 was concerned with the impact of the implementation of the OFI on the (a) missions, (b) recruitment efforts, and (c) admission practices of the State University System (SUS) of Florida public law schools. The following analysis pertains to RQ1a.

The deans and admissions personnel of the participating Florida public law schools were interviewed and asked about any changes in their mission statements. In addition, the mission statements before and after implementation of the OFI were reviewed and compared to determine any impacts.

## University of Florida Fredric G. Levin College of Law (UF)

The longstanding mission statement for UF College of Law is:

> A law school dedicated to advancing human dignity, social welfare and justice through knowledge of the law. Our mission is to obtain excellence in:
>
> 1. Educating professionals
> 2. Advancing legal scholarship
> 3. Serving the public
> 4. Fostering justice
>
> (University of Florida Law School. (2007). Mission Statement of University of Florida College of Law.)

The mission statement remained the same following the OFI. The last revision of the college's mission statement occurred before the OFI Executive Order 99-281 was issued in 1999. Implementation of the OFI did not impact the mission statement of UF College of Law. The mission statement does not appear to address diversity.

## Florida State University College of Law (FSU)

The mission statement of FSU College of Law is lengthy and very detailed. It espouses a mission of preparing its students for the responsible practice of law through a systematic course of instruction. According to the school, its primary purpose for instruction and research is to promote knowledge about the role of legal concepts and values. Its graduates are expected to help shape the growth of the legal profession through their contributions to, among other things, scholarship and public service. The school's faculty is encouraged to support a curriculum of instruction necessary to carry out those goals.

FSU College of Law has divided its mission into three areas that it considers critical to its purpose: teaching, research and scholarship, and service. In teaching, the College seeks to provide students with a diverse curriculum that will instill in them a sense of professional responsibility that leads to good judgment, good ethics, and accurate legal analysis. In addition, the law school faculty is encouraged to engage in research and scholarship through publications in professional journals and papers, and provide mentorship to students and younger faculty. While the college professes to try to positively impact the community at large and engage in public service at all levels, it does not identify any particular segment of the community or society to which it will contribute.

The mission statement has not changed since spring of 2001. Implementation of the OFI did not impact the mission statement of FSU College of Law.

Its mission statement speaks of encouraging a diverse program of study, but it is apparent that the statement is a reference to legal curriculum rather than racial, ethnic and/or cultural diversity. The College also within its mission statements says it seeks to "maximize the opportunity for a diverse student body" but does not suggest how it intends to go about fulfilling this aspect of its mission or exactly what it means by diverse student body, whether it is gender, racial, ethnic, or cultural diversity.

## MINORITY SERVING INSTITUTION: FLORIDA INTERNATIONAL UNIVERSITY COLLEGE OF LAW (FIU)

The FIU College of Law was established by the Florida legislature in 2000 with a particular focus on serving South Floridians, an area with a significant minority population, including Hispanics and Haitians. According to the mission statement, FIU College of Law encourages free discussion of issues among faculty and students and has a healthy respect for differing perspectives. It also expects its faculty, administration, and students to reflect the kind of diverse backgrounds and interests that are evident in the community it serves.

In its mission statement, the school also speaks of a multicultural world and offering students a curriculum that is sensitive to what it calls the "globalization of both public and private law." As a part of its mission, FIU College of Law claims that it seeks to graduate future lawyers who have a desire to help those in need and who appreciate the obligation to serve the community. The College claims to have an obligation to the region, state, nation, and the international community of which it is a part—a clear reference, given the school's location, to serving an ethnically diverse population. Its classroom teachings are intended to promote the University's overall mission as "one of the nation's leading urban public research institutions."

According to officials of the law school, the mission statement has not changed since the school was first established in 2002. Implementation of the OFI did not impact the mission statement of FIU College of Law because the law school did not exist prior to the OFI. The mission statement also mentions diversity as an important function of the institution.

### Minority Serving Institution: Florida Agricultural and Mechanical University College of Law (FAMU)

The mission statement for FAMU College of Law was re-established by the Florida legislature in 2000 after having closed in 1965 and opening the

Florida State University College of Law on its main campus in Tallahassee, Florida. It is located in Orlando, Florida from its previous location on FAMU's main campus in Tallahassee. In summary, its mission is:

> To provide a law program with high academic standards that produces excellent legal professionals who demonstrate professionalism, provide public service, enhance justice and promote scholarship; to provide a program that offers both full-time and part-time learning opportunities to students; and, consistent with the enabling legislation, to provide opportunities for minorities to attain representation within the legal profession. (Mission Statement)

Florida Agricultural and Mechanical University will continue its mission of meeting the educational needs of African Americans and other ethnic minorities, while maintaining its leadership in racial diversity. At the same time, the University seeks students from all racial, ethnic, religious and national groups, without regard to age, sex, or disability, who have the potential to benefit from a sound education. The University provides for all an atmosphere where excellent teaching and lifelong learning are hallmarks.

In law, FAMU reaffirms in its mission statement its historical responsibilities to its students to provide important opportunities for service to the diverse communities in Florida, the nation, and the world. FAMU claims to strive to set, to maintain and to reward high standards for faculty, staff and students through continual evolution and pedagogy, curricula, research and public service demands. FAMU will continue to serve as a beacon of hope and a catalyst for change. The College of Law's role is to promote the development of legal professionals as community leaders who are sensitive to the needs of all people.

The mission statement of FAMU College of Law was not impacted by implementation of the OFI because it did not exist at the time; it had been closed in response to pressure from Supreme Court Chief Justice B.K. Roberts who convinced Florida lawmakers that desegregation had eliminated the need for an all-Black law school. For an in-depth look at the politically-fraught history of FAMU, and the long battle to re-open it as an MSI, see Chapter Three. In its mission statement, the school says it views diversity as an essential aspect of the institution. The FAMU College of Law's mission statement has not been changed since the school reopened its doors in 2002.

## Summary

The mission statements of the SUS of Florida law schools were not impacted by the OFI. The words "diverse," "community," and "multicultural" are interspersed throughout the mission statements of FAMU College of Law and FIU

College of Law. While they were not the only two schools that mentioned diversity within their particular mission statements, they were the only two that spoke with clarity about diversity having a cultural and ethnic connotation. FSU College of Law's mission statement mentions the word diverse three times, but in rather ambiguous terms with no reference to whether it means gender, age, racial, cultural, or ethnic diversity. UF College of Law, in its mission statement, acknowledges neither the importance of nor a desire for diversity.

## IMPACT OF OFI ON LAW SCHOOL ADMISSION PRACTICES

Research question 1 also sought to determine the impact of the implementation of the OFI on the (b) recruitment efforts and (c) admission practices of the SUS of Florida public law schools. The deans and admissions personnel of the SUS of Florida public law schools were interviewed to determine the impact of implementation of the OFI on their recruitment and admissions practices.

### University of Florida Fredric G. Levin College of Law (UF)

Participants 1 and 2 indicated that the OFI did not impact recruitment or admissions practices. Participant 1 expressed some degree of discomfort with attempting to answer this question. This particular individual said that they were not able to speak definitively to this question due to not being at the college in 1999.

### Florida State University College of Law (FSU)

Participant 3 and 4 indicated that the OFI had some impact on either their school's recruitment or admissions practices. The College of Law, they said, made appropriate adjustments to its recruitment or admissions practices in order to conform to the OFI. One respondent informed the researcher that race may not be taken into account in making admission decisions, but it may be used in recruitment efforts.

### Minority Serving Institution: Florida International University College of Law (FIU)

Participant 5 believed implementation of the OFI affected the school "probably not at all." The law school continues to recruit minority students at

HBCUs and other institutions with high minority enrollment as a normal part of their recruitment efforts and not because of the OFI. The FIU College of Law did not exist prior to the OFI; however, as a result of supporting powers, the institution was established.

### Minority Serving Institution: Florida Agricultural and Mechanical University College of Law (FAMU)

Representatives from the FAMU College of Law did not respond, but the school did not exist prior to the OFI because its doors had been closed by the state's legislature many years earlier. As mentioned in an earlier chapter on the historical context of the OFI, political forces in the state may have led to the reopening of this institution as a result of legislative maneuverings to help ensure approval of the OFI. FAMU law school officials declined to participate in the study, and while no specific reason was given, the staff turnover at the time of inquiry may have contributed to the decision not to respond.

### Summary

While some participants determined that the OFI did not impact recruitment or admission practices, others suggested that they made changes to their recruitment efforts or recruitment practices in an effort to comply with Executive Order 99-281. One participant expressed that the OFI allows the use of race as a factor in recruitment but prohibits the use of race as a factor in admission decisions. Another respondent speculated that implementation of the OFI has had no impact on the school since they normally recruit at institutions with high minority enrollment.

## IMPACT OF CREATION OF MSI ON LAW SCHOOL MISSION STATEMENTS

Research question 2 sought to determine the impact of the MSI law schools on the (a) mission statements, (b) recruitment efforts and (c) admission practices of the SUS of Florida public law schools. These newly established law schools were legislated and implemented during the same timeframe of the OFI.

The mission statements were obtained, reviewed, and compared to determine the impact. Interview questions were directed to the deans and admissions personnel of the SUS of Florida public law schools regarding the mission statements before and after the creation of the MSI law schools. The following analysis pertains to RQ2a.

## University of Florida Fredric G. Levin College of Law (UF)

Participants 1 and 2 suggested that their institution's mission statement had not been revised since the two new law schools were created. Their responses implied that the addition of the two MSI law schools did not impact their school's mission statement. While the mission statement of the law school was not affected by the addition of two new MSI law schools, Participant 2 suggested that the creation of the two law schools may have been the reason Florida's legislature abandoned two state programs to promote minority enrollment in law schools. The two programs, the Minority Participation in Legal Education (MPLE) and Virgil Hawkins Scholarship, were ended by Florida lawmakers in close proximity to the implementation of the Executive Order 99-281 and the MSI Law Schools.

## Florida State University College of Law (FSU)

Participants 3 and 4 indicated that the addition of the MSI law schools did not impact their school's mission statement. Therefore, the mission statements did not change. Both respondents had knowledge of how the two MSI law schools were created, which was by act of the Florida Legislature with passage of Senate Bill 68.

## Minority Serving Institution: Florida International University College of Law (FIU)

Participant 5 implied that the creation of MSI law schools did have an impact on the institution's mission statement. As a result of the mission given to the school when it was created, its mission statement includes a commitment to diversity. The institution is committed to providing underrepresented minorities with access to the legal profession. The law school's purpose, as outlined in its mission statement, makes several references to multiculturalism and diversity:

> The student body, faculty and administration reflect a wide variety of backgrounds and interests. Out of this diversity, the College of Law seeks to create a scholarly community in which students and faculty discuss issues freely and with respect for differing perspectives. (Florida International University Law School. (2007). Mission Statement of Florida International University Law School.) Retrieved March 26, 2007.

### Minority Serving Institution: Florida Agricultural and Mechanical University College of Law (FAMU)

The FAMU College of Law elected not to participate in the study. Similar to FIU College of Law, FAMU College of Law makes wide reference to diversity in its mission statement, proclaiming for example:

> To provide opportunities for minorities to attain representation within the legal profession. Florida Agricultural and Mechanical University will continue its mission of meeting the educational needs of African Americans and other ethnic minorities, while maintaining its leadership in racial diversity. At the same time, the University seeks students from all racial, ethnic, religious and national groups. (Florida State University College of Law. (2007). Mission of Florida State University College of Law.) Retrieved March 26, 2007.

### Summary

Two of the institutions that responded to the interview questions said that the addition of the two MSI law schools did not impact their mission statements. One of the participants, speaking as a representative of one of the law schools that had been created, said the institution remains true to its founding principle, a commitment to diversity and providing access to minorities.

## IMPACT OF CREATION OF MSIS ON LAW SCHOOL ADMISSION PRACTICES

Research question 2 also sought to determine the impacts of the creation of MSI law schools on the (b) recruitment efforts and (c) admission practices of the SUS of Florida public law schools. Deans and admissions personnel of the SUS of Florida public law schools were interviewed and documents were examined. Three of the four colleges of law agreed to participate in the study, while the fourth declined to respond.

### University of Florida Fredric G. Levin College of Law (UF)

Participants 1 and 2 suggested that the creation of the two MSI law schools did not impact the recruitment efforts and admission practices of the law school. They added, however, that certain recruitment efforts were revised, improved, and strengthened to intentionally increase diversity. While some admission practices were changed, these revisions, improvements, and changes were not the result of the creation of two new public law schools.

### Florida State University College of Law (FSU)

Participants 3 and 4 revealed that the addition of the MSI law schools did not impact the recruitment efforts or admission practices of their law school. The criteria regarding their admission decisions for the institution only changed in an effort to conform to implementation of the OFI and not as a result of the two MSI law schools. Recruitment practices, according to participant 3, did not change after creation of FIU and FAMU Colleges of Law.

### Minority Serving Institution: Florida International University College of Law (FIU)

As would be expected, considering its status as one of the MSI law schools in question, Participant 5 said that the creation of MSI law schools in Florida has been very important to their institution's recruitment efforts and admission practices. The participant considered the fact that the institution was an MSI to be central to all that the school does with regard to recruitment and admission policies.

### Minority Serving Institution: Florida Agricultural and Mechanical University College of Law (FAMU)

The FAMU College of Law did not respond to the study.

### Summary

Two of the four institutions indicated that creation of MSI colleges of law did not impact law school admission practices at their particular institutions. One of the MSI law schools concluded that the creation of FIU has been central to all that the school does with regard to recruitment and admission practices. However, another institution indicated that their particular law school's admission practices were not impacted as a result of the creation of the MSI law schools, but was impacted as a result of the OFI.

## IMPACT OF OFI ON LAW SCHOOLS' STUDENT DIVERSITY

Research question 3 focused on the impact of the implementation of the OFI on the diversity of student (a) applicants, (b) admissions, (c) enrollment, and (d) LSAT scores. Given the quantitative nature of this question, four null: Ho and their associated alternative: Ha hypotheses were proposed and tested. Hypotheses 3a, 3b, and 3c were tested using the Z-test of proportion. The fourth hypothesis (3d) involved the comparison of pre- and post-OFI mean LSAT scores and was tested using a one-way analysis of variance (ANOVA). The following discussion summarizes the findings for each of these four pairs of null and alternative hypotheses.

Ho3a: There is no significant difference in the percentage of minority applicants to the public law schools following implementation of the OFI in 1999.

Ha3a: There is a significant difference in the percentage of minority applicants to the public law schools following implementation of the OFI in 1999.

There was a significant jump in the percentage of minority applicants to the public law schools in Florida prior to and following the implementation of the OFI (See table 5.1), followed by a significant drop in percentage. The schools, however, maintained ahead of where they initially began. An examination of the data indicated an increase in the percentage of minority applicants between 1998–1999 (25.53 percent) and the two subsequent academic years: 1999–2000 (29.26 percent), $z = 3.73$, $p < .01$; and 2000–2001 (29.85 percent), $z = 4.32$, $p < .01$. The only exceptions were in the change in percentages between academic years 1998–1999 and 2001–2002 when there was a non-significant decline in the percentage of minority applicants (1.79 percentage points), 1999–2000 to 2000–2001 and 1999–2000 to 2001–2002. Thus, Hypothesis 3a was rejected, and it was concluded that there was a significant difference in the percentage of minority applicants to the public law schools following implementation of the OFI. This increase in the percentage of minority applicants has been maintained through the 2005–2006 academic year.

Ho3b: There is no significant difference in the percentage of minorities admitted to the public law schools following implementation of the OFI.

**Table 5.1. Comparison of the Percentage of Minority Applicants to the Public Law Schools Prior to and Following Implementation of OFI**

| *Academic Year* | *Percentage Minority Applicants* | *1998-1999 (Percentage Points Difference)* | *1999–2000 (Percentage Points Difference)* | *2000–2001 (Percentage Points Difference)* |
|---|---|---|---|---|
| 1998–1999 | 25.53 | — | — | — |
| 1999–2000 | 29.26 | 3.73** | — | — |
| 2000–2001 | 29.85 | 4.32** | .59 | — |
| 2001–2002 | 27.32 | 1.79 | –1.94 | –2.53* |
| 2002–2003 | 34.51 | 8.98** | 5.25** | 4.65** |
| 2003–2004 | 35.98 | 10.45** | 6.72** | 6.13** |
| 2004–2005 | 34.46 | 8.93** | 4.76** | 3.60** |
| 2005–2006 | 36.02 | 10.49** | 6.76** | 6.17** |

*p < .05, **p < .01

Ha3b: There is a significant difference in the percentage of minorities admitted to the public law schools following implementation of the OFI.

There was a significant change in the percentage of minority applicants accepted to the public law schools in Florida prior to and following the implementation of the OFI (See table 5.2).

**Table 5.2. Comparison of the Percentage of Minority Applicants Accepted to the Public Law Schools Prior to and Following Implementation of OFI**

| *Academic Year* | *Percentage Minority Applicants* | *1998–1999 (Percentage Points Difference)* | *1999–2000 (Percentage Points Difference)* | *2000–2001 (Percentage Points Difference)* |
|---|---|---|---|---|
| 1998–1999 | 23.14 | — | — | — |
| 1999–2000 | 27.76 | 4.62** | — | — |
| 2000–2001 | 27.72 | 4.58** | –.04 | — |
| 2001–2002 | 25.32 | 2.17 | –2.44 | –2.40 |
| 2002–2003 | 27.43 | 4.28** | –.33 | –.29 |
| 2003–2004 | 30.24 | 7.10** | 2.48 | 2.50 |
| 2004–2005 | 29.56 | 6.42** | .38 | .42 |
| 2005–2006 | 31.22 | 8.07** | 3.46** | 3.50** |

*p < .05, **p < .01

An examination of the data indicated an increase in the percentage of minority applicants admitted to the law schools between the academic year 1998–1999 (23.14 percent) and 1999–2000 (27.76 percent), $z = 4.62$, $p < .01$. For example, 23.14 percent of the students admitted to the law schools in 1998–1999 were from racial and ethnic minorities. The OFI was signed by Governor Bush in 1999. However, the percentage of minorities admitted jumped to 27.76 percent in 1999–2000 and 27.72 percent in 2000–2001. With a slight non-significant decrease (-2.44) in 2001–2002, the numbers continued to increase and reached 31.22 percent by 2005–2006. The only exception to the significant increases was a non-significant decline in the percentage of minority applicants (2.17 percentage points) between 1998 and 2001. Thus, Hypothesis 3b was rejected, and it was concluded that there was a significant difference in the percentage of minority students admitted to the public law schools following implementation of the OFI. This increase in percentage of minority students admitted to the law schools has been maintained through the 2005–2006 academic year.

Ho3c: There is no significant difference in the percentage of minorities enrolled at the public law schools following implementation of the OFI.

Ha3c: There is a significant difference in the percentage of minorities enrolled at the public law schools following implementation of the OFI.

There was a significant change in the percentage of minority students who enrolled in the public law schools in Florida prior to and following the implementation of the OFI (See table 5.3). An examination of the data indicated an increase in the percentage of minority students enrolled at the public law schools for the comparisons between the academic years 1998–1999 (23.91 percent) and 1999–2000 (28.08 percent), $z = 4.17$, $p < .01$.

**Table 5.3. Comparison of the Percentage of Minority Students Enrolled at Public Law School Prior to and Following Implementation of OFI**

| *Academic Year* | *Percentage Minority Enrolled* | *1998–1999 (Percentage Points Difference)* | *1999–2000 (Percentage Points Difference)* | *2000–2001 (Percentage Points Difference* |
|---|---|---|---|---|
| 1998–1999 | 23.91 | — | — | — |
| 1999–2000 | 28.08 | 4.17** | — | — |
| 2000–2001 | 26.49 | 2.58** | -1.59 | — |
| 2001–2002 | 24.64 | .73 | -3.44 | -1.85 |
| 2002–2003 | 27.18 | 3.27** | -.90 | .69 |
| 2003–2004 | 32.43 | 8.52** | 4.35 | 5.94 |
| 2004–2005 | 31.12 | 7.21** | 2.82 | 4.41 |
| 2005–2006 | 34.02 | 10.11** | 5.94** | 7.53** |

*p < .05, **p < .01

For example, 23.91 percent of the students enrolled in 1998–1999 were from racial and ethnic minorities. After Governor Bush signed the OFI in 1999, the percentage of minorities enrolled increased to 28.08 percent in 1999–2000 and 26.49 percent in 2000–2001. With a slight decrease in 2001–2002 to 24.64 percent, the numbers rebounded to 27.18 percent in 2002–2003 and have remained at about 31 percent since 2002–2004. Thus, Hypothesis 3c was rejected, and it was concluded that there was a significant difference in the percentage of minority students enrolled at Florida's public law schools following implementation of the OFI.

Ho3d: There is no significant difference in the average LSAT scores of the public law schools following implementation of the OFI.

Ha3d: There is a significant difference in the average LSAT scores of the public law schools following implementation of the OFI.

A non-significant difference was found in the mean LSAT scores of law school students attending the public law schools following implementation of the OFI, $F(4, 58) = .843$, $p > .05$ (See table 5.4). The mean LSAT scores remained relatively unchanged during this period.

**Table 5.4. ANOVA Results for Impact of OFI on LSAT Scores**

| *Source* | *Type III Sum of Squares* | *df* | *Mean Square* | *F* | *Sig.* |
|---|---|---|---|---|---|
| Year | 79.407 | 4 | 19.852 | .843 | .504 |
| Error | 1365.672 | 58 | 23.546 | | |
| Total | 1464607.000 | 63 | | | |
| Corrected Total | 1445.079 | 62 | | | |

R Squared = .055 (Adjusted R Squared = -.010)

## IMPACT OF OFI ON THE DIVERSITY OF FLORIDA'S LEGAL PROFESSION

Research question 4 focused on the impact of implementation of the OFI on the diversity of Florida's legal profession (graduates and those admitted to the Florida Bar). Given the quantitative nature of this question, two null: Ho and their associated alternative: Ha hypotheses were proposed and tested. The following discussion summarizes the findings for each of these two pairs of null and alternative hypotheses.

Ho4a: There is no significant difference in the percentage of minority graduates at the public law schools following implementation of the OFI.

Ha4a: There is a significant difference in the percentage of minority graduates at the public law schools following implementation of the OFI.

There was a non-significant change in the percentage of minority graduates of the public law schools in Florida prior to and following implementation of the OFI (See table 5.5). An examination of the data indicated that

**Table 5.5. Comparison of the Percentage of Minority Graduates of Public Law Schools Prior to and Following Implementation of OFI**

| *Academic Year* | *Percentage Minority Graduates* | *1998–1999 (Percentage Points Difference)* | *1999–2000 (Percentage Points Difference)* | *2000–2001 (Percentage Points Difference)* |
|---|---|---|---|---|
| 1997–1998 | 23.34 | — | — | — |
| 1998–1999 | 25.90 | 2.56 | — | — |
| 1999–2000 | 22.00 | −1.34 | — | — |
| 2000–2001 | 23.84 | .05 | −1.59 | — |
| 2001–2002 | 27.73 | 4.39 | −3.44 | −1.85 |
| 2002–2003 | 26.27 | 2.93 | −.90 | .69 |
| 2003–2004 | 27.29 | 3.95 | 4.35 | 5.94 |
| 2004–2005 | 22.29 | −.03 | 282 | 4.41 |
| 2005–2006 | 29.09 | 5.75** | 5.94** | 7.53** |

*p < .05, **p < .01

the percentage of minority graduates has fluctuated between 22.00 percent and 29.09 percent since the signing of the OFI. The comparison between the percentage of minority graduates in the 1998–1999 graduating class (25.90 percent minority graduates) and the percentage of minority graduates in the 2001–2002 graduating class (27.73 percent), the first graduating class to be potentially impacted by OFI, was not significant. The first significant change in the percentage of minority graduates did not occur until 2005–2006, the second year in which there were also graduates from the MSI law schools. Thus, Hypothesis 4a was not rejected, and it was concluded that there was not a significant difference in the percentage of minority graduates of Florida's public law schools following implementation of the OFI.

Ho4b: There is no significant difference in the percentage of minority law school graduates sitting for the Florida Bar Examination following implementation of the OFI.

Ha4b: There is a significant difference in the percentage of minority law school graduates sitting for the Florida Bar Examination following implementation of the OFI.

This hypothesis could not be tested because the FBA indicated that they could not release this information. The data received from the FBA was the percentage of practicing attorneys who are members of the Florida Bar, which is found in table 5.6.

**Table 5.6. Percentage of Attorneys by Race Certified by the Florida Bar Association**

| *Year* | *White* | *Hispanic* | *African American* | *Other* |
|---|---|---|---|---|
| 1996 | 92 | 5 | 2 | 1 |
| 1998 | 91 | 6 | 2 | 1 |
| 2000 | 91 | 6 | 2 | 1 |
| 2002 | 90 | 7 | 2 | 1 |
| 2004 | 89 | 7 | 2 | 2 |
| 2006 | 89 | 7 | 2 | 2 |
| Current | 85 | 9 | 3 | 3 |

*Source:* The Florida Bar 2006 Economics and Law Office Management Survey

The percentage increase of minorities ranged from 8 percent to 15 percent from 1998 to 2006. There was a five to nine percentage point increase for Hispanics, a two to three percentage point increase for African Americans, and an increase of one to three percentage points for Native Americans and Asian Americans.

## IMPACT OF THE CREATION OF MSI LAW SCHOOLS ON STUDENT DIVERSITY

Research question 5 focused on the impact of the creation of MSI law schools and their impact on the (a) diversity of student applicants, (b) admissions, (c) enrollment, and (d) LSAT scores. Given the quantitative nature of this question, four null: Ho and their associated alternative: Ha hypotheses were proposed and tested. The following discussion summarizes the findings for each of these four pairs of null and alternative hypotheses.

Ho5a: There is no significant difference in the percentage of minority applicants to the public law schools following the creation of MSI law schools in 2002.

Ha5a: There is a significant difference in the percentage of minority applicants to the public law schools following the creation of MSI law schools.

There was a significant change in the percentage of minority applicants to the public law schools in Florida prior to and following the creation of the MSIs (See table 5.7).

**Table 5.7. Comparison of the Percentage of Minority Applicants to the Public Law Schools Prior to and Following the Creation of the Minority Serving Institutions**

| *Academic Year* | *Percentage Minority Applicants* | *2002–2003 (Percentage Points Difference)* | *2003–2004 (Percentage Points Difference)* | *2004–2005 (Percentage Points Difference)* |
|---|---|---|---|---|
| 1998–1999 | 25.53 | — | — | — |
| 1999–2000 | 29.26 | — | — | — |
| 2000–2001 | 29.85 | — | — | — |
| 2001–2002 | 27.32 | — | — | — |
| 2002–2003 | 34.51 | 7.19** | — | — |
| 2003–2004 | 35.98 | 8.66** | 1.47 | — |
| 2004–2005 | 34.46 | 7.14** | –.05 | –1.52 |
| 2005–2006 | 36.02 | 8.70** | 1.51 | .04 |

*p < .05, **p < .01

An examination of the data indicated an increase in the percentage of minority applicants for the comparisons between the academic years 2001–2002 (27.32 percent); 2002–2003 (34.51 percent), $z = 7.19$, $p < .01$; and 2003–2004 (35.98 percent), $z = 8.66$, $p < .01$. The only exceptions were the non-significant change in percentages between academic years 2002–2003, which was 34.51 percent, and 2004–2005, which was 34.42 percent. Thus, Hypothesis 5a was rejected, and it was concluded that there was a significant difference in the percentage of minority applicants to the public law schools following the creation of MSIs. This increase in the percentage of minority applicants has been maintained through the 2005–2006 academic year with 36.02 percent minorities and a significant change of 8.70.

Ho5b: There is no significant difference in the percentage of minorities admitted to the public law schools following the creation of MSI law schools.

Ha5b: There is a significant difference in the percentage of minorities admitted to the public law schools following the creation of MSI law schools.

There was a significant change in the percentage of minorities admitted to the public law schools in Florida prior to and following the creation of MSIs (See table 5.8). An examination of the data indicated an increase in the percentage of minorities admitted to the law schools for the comparisons between the academic year 2001–2002 (25.32 percent) and the academic years 2002–2003 (27.43 percent) and 2003–2004 (30.24 percent), $z = 4.92$, $p < .01$. For example, 27.43 percent of the students admitted to the law schools in 2002–2003 were from racial and ethnic minorities following the creation of MSIs in 2002. The percentage of minorities rose to 30.24 percent in 2003–2004 and decreased slightly in 2004–2005 to 29.56 percent. However, the percentage of minorities continued to increase in 2005-2006 to 31.22 percent. Thus, Hypothesis 5b was rejected, and it was concluded that there was a significant difference in the percentage of minority students accepted to the public law schools following the creation of MSIs. The creation of the MSI institutions did increase the percentage of minority students admitted to Florida's public law schools. The increase in the percentage of minority students admitted to the law schools has been maintained through the 2005–2006 academic year. Given the missions of the MSI institutions and the expanded number of slots in the public law schools, this finding is not surprising.

**Table 5.8. Comparison of the Percentage of Minority Applicants Accepted to the Public Law Schools Prior to and Following the Creation of the Minority Serving Institutions**

| *Academic Year* | *Percentage Minority Accepted* | *2002–2003 (Percentage Points Difference)* | *2003–2004 (Percentage Points Difference)* | *2004–2005 (Percentage Points Difference)* |
|---|---|---|---|---|
| 1998–1999 | 23.14 | — | — | — |
| 1999–2000 | 27.76 | — | — | — |
| 2000–2001 | 27.72 | — | — | — |
| 2001–2002 | 25.32 | — | — | — |
| 2002–2003 | 27.43 | 2.11 | — | — |
| 2003–2004 | 30.24 | 4.92** | 2.91 | — |
| 2004–2005 | 29.56 | 4.24** | 2.13 | –.68 |
| 2005–2006 | 31.22 | 5.90** | 3.79* | .98 |

*p < .05, **p < .01

Ho5c: There is no significant difference in the percentage of minorities enrolled at the public law schools following the creation of MSI law schools.

Ha5c: There is a significant difference in the percentage of minorities enrolled at the public law schools following the creation of MSI law schools.

There was a significant change in the percentage of minority students who enrolled in the public law schools in Florida prior to and following the creation of MSIs (See table 5.9). An examination of the data indicated an increase in the percentage of minority students enrolled at the public law schools for the comparisons between the academic years 2001–2002 (24.64 percent), 2002–2003 (27.18 percent), and 2003–2004 (32.43 percent), $z = 5.79$, $p < .01$. For example, 27.18 percent of the students enrolled in 2002-2003 were from racial and ethnic minorities. Following the creation of MSI law schools, the percentage of minorities enrolled increased to 32.43 percent in 2003–2004, with a slight decrease in 2004–2005 to 31.12 percent, and an increase to 34.02 percent in 2005–2006. Thus, Hypothesis 5c was rejected, and it was concluded that there was a significant difference in the percentage of minority students enrolled at Florida's public law schools following the creation of MSIs. Again, this finding supports the intent and mission of the MSI institutions. The percentage of minority students enrolled in the public law schools could be higher if a greater percentage of the minority students admitted to the public law schools actually enrolled.

Ho5d: There is no significant difference in the average LSAT scores of the public law schools following the creation of MSI law schools.

Ha5d: There is a significant difference in the average LSAT scores of the public law schools following the creation of MSI law schools.

**Table 5.9. Comparison of the Percentage of Minority Students Enrolled at Public Law Schools Prior to and Following the Creation of the Minority Serving Institutions**

| *Academic Year* | *Percentage Minority Enrolled* | *2002–2003 (Percentage Points Difference)* | *2003–2004 (Percentage Points Difference)* | *2004–2005 (Percentage Points Difference)* |
|---|---|---|---|---|
| 1998–1999 | 23.91 | — | — | — |
| 1999–2000 | 28.08 | — | — | — |
| 2000–2001 | 26.49 | — | — | — |
| 2001–2002 | 24.64 | — | — | — |
| 2002–2003 | 27.18 | 2.54 | — | — |
| 2003–2004 | 32.43 | 5.79** | 5.25 | — |
| 2004–2005 | 31.12 | 6.48** | 3.94 | –1.31 |
| 2005–2006 | 34.02 | 9.38** | 6.87** | 1.59 |

*p < .05, **p < .01

Consistent with the findings from Hypothesis 3d, which concerned LSAT scores following the implementation of the OFI, a non-significant difference was found in the mean LSAT scores of law school students following the creation of MSI law schools, $F(5, 106) = 1.065$, $p > .05$ (See table 5.10). The mean LSAT scores remained relatively unchanged during this period.

**Table 5.10. ANOVA Results for the Creation of MSI Law Schools on LSAT Scores**

| *Source* | *Type III Sum of Squares* | *Df* | *Mean Square* | *F* | *Sig.* |
|---|---|---|---|---|---|
| Year | 104.30 | 5 | 20.861 | .1065 | .384 |
| Error | 2077.13 | 106 | 19.596 | | |
| Corrected Total | 2181.43 | 111 | | | |

R Squared = .055 (Adjusted R Squared = -.010)

## IMPACT OF THE CREATION OF MSI LAW SCHOOLS ON THE DIVERSITY OF FLORIDA'S LEGAL PROFESSION

Research question 6 focused on the impact of the creation of MSI law schools and their impact on the diversity of Florida's legal profession (graduates and those admitted to the Florida Bar). Given the quantitative nature of this question, two null: Ho and their associated alternative: Ha hypotheses were proposed and tested. The following discussion summarizes the findings for each of these two hypotheses.

Ho6a: There is no significant difference in the percentage of minority graduates at the public law schools following the creation of MSI law schools.

Ha6a: There is a significant difference in the percentage of minority graduates at the public law schools following the creation of MSI law schools.

There was a non-significant change in the percentage of minority graduates of the public law schools in Florida prior to and following the creation of MSIs (See able 5.11). An examination of the data indicated that the percentage of minority graduates was 27.73 percent in 2001–2002 and 26.27 percent in 2002–2003, the academic year the MSI law schools opened. The percentage of minority graduates actually decreased to 22.99 percent in 2004–2005, the academic year for the first graduating class. The difference between the percentage of minority graduates prior to the creation of the MSI laws schools and the first two years in which there were graduates of the MSI laws schools was not significant; however, the comparison between 2004–2005 (22.99 percent) and 2005–2006 (29.09 percent) was significant. The reason for this significant difference may be due to a decline in the percentage of minority graduates in 2004–2005, which appears to be part of the regular variability in the percentage of minority graduates when examined over five to ten years. Thus, Hypothesis 6a was not rejected, and it was concluded that there was not a significant difference in the percentage of minority graduates of Florida's public law schools following the creation of MSI law schools.

**Table 5.11. Comparison of the Percentage of Minority Graduates at Public Law Schools Prior to and Following the Creation of Minority Serving Institutions**

| *Academic Year* | *Percentage Minority Graduates* | *2004–2005 (Percentage Points Difference)* | *2005–2006 (Percentage Points Difference)* |
|---|---|---|---|
| 1997–1998 | 23.34 | — | — |
| 1998–1999 | 25.90 | — | — |
| 1999–2000 | 22.00 | — | — |
| 2000–2001 | 23.84 | — | — |
| 2001–2002 | 27.73 | — | — |
| 2002–2003 | 26.27 | — | — |
| 2003–2004 | 27.29 | — | — |
| 2004–2005 | 22.99 | -3.28 | — |
| 2005–2006 | 29.09 | 2.82 | 6.10** |

$*p < .05$, $**p < .01$

Ho6b: There is no significant difference in the percentage of minority law school graduates sitting for the Florida Bar Examination following the creation of MSI law schools.

Ha6b: There is a significant difference in the percentage of minority law school graduates sitting for the Florida Bar Examination following the creation of MSI law schools.

This hypothesis could not be tested because the FBA indicated that it could not release this information. The data received from the FBA yielded the percentage of practicing attorneys who are members of the Florida Bar (See table 5.6). The percentage of minorities hovered between 8 percent and 15 percent from 1998 to 2006.

## CHAPTER SUMMARY

In determining the impact of the OFI, as well as the opening of two MSI law schools on diversity in Florida's publicly funded law schools, this research examined the way these schools recruited and admitted students. The results of this portion of the study were inconclusive. For example, the OFI appears to have had no impact on the four public law schools' missions, as indicated by their mission statements. Where there was no mention of diversity in the law schools' mission statements prior to implementation of the OFI, there was the same absence of attention to diversity in the years that followed the OFI. Likewise, the creation of two MSI law schools had no apparent impact on the schools' mission statements. Florida State University and The University of Florida law schools were present prior to the OFI being implemented. Florida A&M University and Florida International University law schools opened in 2002, one academic year after the implementation of the OFI.

The results were also mixed when this study queried law school deans and admissions personnel about the impact the OFI had on their schools' admission and recruitment practices. Half of the law schools indicated that their admission practices had changed in order to comply with OFI and its race neutral mandates, while the other half of the law schools said their policies had not changed since neither was open prior to implementation of the OFI. A participant from one institution suggested that there was no impact because they normally recruit at schools with large minority populations. This was an interesting observation since, as one respondent pointed out, the OFI does not require race neutral policies for recruitment practices, only for admission decisions. Overall, none of the respondents believed that the creation of two MSI law schools had any major impact on their admission or recruitment policies.

There are areas in which implementation of the OFI seems to have had a significant impact, including the percentage of minorities applying and being admitted to Florida's public law schools. With but a few years when there were non-significant declines in the percentage of minority law school applicants, there was an overall increase each year since 1999 when the OFI was implemented, and that increase continued through 2006. Moreover, the percentage of minority students admitted to the four public law schools rose immediately after the OFI and has increased in most years since, from nearly 28 percent in the 1999–2000 academic year to more than 31 percent in 2005–2006.

This study found there to be a non-significant difference in pre- and post-OFI mean LSAT scores of students who attended public law schools in Florida following implementation of the OFI. Likewise, a non-significant difference was discovered in the percentage of minority graduates from these institutions before or after the creation of two MSI law schools. This research was not able to ascertain whether there were any differences in the percentage of minority law school graduates sitting for the Florida Bar Exam before and after implementation of the OFI or before and after creation of the two minority-serving law schools in the state because of the FBA's inability to release the requested data.

# *Chapter Six*

# Discussion

The intent of this study was to determine what, if any, impact the OFI and the simultaneous addition of two MSI law schools had on diversity in Florida's public law schools and, therefore, on the state's legal profession. It was anticipated that the research would provide additional insight into administrative and legislative policies on racial and ethnic diversity and whether those policies accomplished their stated goals. This study yielded rich results that could be helpful in predicting the impact of policies promoted to improve diversity in academic law programs and organizations. The results are grouped and discussed under each of the two qualitative and four quantitative research questions.

## IMPACT OF OFI ON LAW SCHOOL MISSION STATEMENTS

The mission statements of the SUS of Florida law schools were not impacted by the OFI. The words "diverse," "community," and "multicultural" are interspersed throughout the mission statements of FAMU College of Law and FIU College of Law. While they were not the only two schools that mentioned diversity within their particular mission statements, they were the only two that spoke with clarity about diversity having a cultural and ethnic connotation. FSU College of Law's mission statement mentions the word diverse three times, but in rather ambiguous terms with no reference to whether it means gender, age, racial, cultural, or ethnic diversity. UF College of Law, in its mission statement, acknowledges neither the importance of nor a desire for diversity.

FAMU and FIU Colleges of Law both mention diversity in their mission statements. While they are alone among Florida's four public law schools to speak of the importance of diversity in their stated missions, they were created as MSIs, therefore their mission being to include diversity by definition. FIU College of Law says in its mission statement, “Out of this diversity, the College of Law seeks to create a scholarly community in which students and faculty discuss issues freely and with respect for differing perspectives.” FAMU College of Law also speaks of diversity in its mission statement, which says, “In law, FAMU reaffirms its historical responsibilities to its students to provide important opportunities for service to the diverse communities in Florida, the nation, and the world.” This, however, does not represent a change in either school’s mission statement, but rather, a restatement of the mission for which each law school believes it was created.

## IMPACT OF OFI ON LAW SCHOOL ADMISSION PRACTICES

Three of the four public law schools in Florida agreed to participate in the study, while a fourth law school declined to respond to the questionnaire. The three deans and three admissions personnel were interviewed to determine the impact of implementation of the OFI on their recruitment and admission practices. While some respondents determined that the OFI did not impact recruitment or admission practices, others suggested that they made changes to their recruitment efforts or recruitment practices in an effort to comply with Executive Order 99-281.

Three of the respondents reported that the OFI had no impact on recruitment or admission practices of their schools. However, two respondents suggested that they made changes or adjustments to their recruitment efforts and admission practices in an effort to bring their institutions into compliance with the executive order. Another respondent suggested that there was no need to change their school’s recruitment practices because while the OFI excludes the use of race as a factor in admission decisions, it permits the use of race as a factor in recruitment practices. Another respondent said the school already recruits at minority institutions but it does so as a result of its stated mission and not because of the OFI.

## IMPACT OF CREATION OF MSIS ON LAW SCHOOL MISSION STATEMENTS

All of the institutions that responded to the questionnaire said that the addition of two MSI law schools did not impact their mission statements. One of the respondents from the two law schools that had been created simultaneously with the implementation of OFI said the institution remains true to its founding principle, a commitment to diversity and providing access to minorities.

## IMPACT OF CREATION OF MSI ON LAW SCHOOL ADMISSION PRACTICES

Three of the four institutions indicated that creation of the two MSI colleges of law did not impact law school admission practices at their particular institutions. One of the MSI's (FIU) stated that the creation of the law school was central to all that FIU does with regard to recruitment and admission practices. However, another institution indicated that their particular law school's admission practices was impacted as a result of the OFI.

## IMPACT OF OFI ON LAW SCHOOL'S STUDENT DIVERSITY

Student Applicants: There was a significant change in the percentage of minority applicants to the public law schools in Florida prior to and following implementation of the OFI (See table 5.1). An examination of the data indicated an increase in the percentage of minority applicants. This increase in the percentage of minority applicants was maintained through the 2005–2006 academic year.

Minority Students Admitted: There was a significant change in the percentage of minority applicants accepted to the public law schools in Florida prior to and following implementation of the OFI (See table 5.2). An examination of the data indicated an increase in the percentage of minority applicants admitted to the law schools. For example, 23.14 percent of the students admitted to the law schools in 1998–1999 were from racial and ethnic minorities. With a slight decrease in 2001–2002, the numbers continued to increase and reached 31.22 percent by 2005–2006. Thus, it was concluded that there was a significant difference in the percentage of minority students admitted to the public law schools following implementation of the OFI.

Minority Students Enrolled: There was a significant change in the percentage of minority students who enrolled in the public law schools in Florida prior to and following implementation of the OFI (See table 5.3). An examination of the data indicated an increase in the percentage of minority students enrolled at the public law schools. Thus, it was concluded that there was a significant difference in the percentage of minority students enrolled at Florida's public law schools following implementation of the OFI.

LSAT Scores: A non-significant difference was found in the mean LSAT scores of law school students attending the public law schools following implementation of the OFI, $F(4, 58) = .843$, $p > .05$ (See table 5.4) . The mean LSAT scores remained relatively unchanged during this period.

## IMPACT OF OFI ON THE DIVERSITY OF FLORIDA'S LEGAL PROFESSION: GRADUATES AND THOSE ADMITTED TO THE BAR

Minority Graduates: There was a non-significant change in the percentage of minority graduates of the public law schools in Florida prior to and following implementation of the OFI (See table 5.5). Thus, it was concluded that there was not a significant difference in the percentage of minority graduates of Florida's public law schools following implementation of the OFI.

Minority Florida Bar Examination: This hypothesis could not be tested because the FBA indicated that it could not release this information. The data received from the FBA was related to the percentage of practicing attorneys who are members of the Florida Bar (See table 5.6).

## IMPACT OF THE CREATION OF MSI LAW SCHOOLS ON STUDENT DIVERSITY

Minority Serving Law Schools and Minority Applicants: There was a significant change in the percentage of minority applicants to the public law schools in Florida prior to and following the creation of the MSIs (See table 5.7). An examination of the data indicated an increase in the percentage of minority applicants. Thus, it was concluded that there was a significant difference in the percentage of minority applicants to the public law schools following the creation of MSIs.

Minority Serving Law Schools and Minority Admissions: There was a significant change in the percentage of minorities admitted to the public law schools in Florida prior to and following the creation of MSIs (See table 5.8). An examination of the data indicated an increase in the percentage of minorities admitted to the law schools. Thus, it was concluded that there was a significant difference in the percentage of minority students accepted to the public law schools following the creation of MSIs. The increased percentage of minority students admitted to the law schools has been maintained through the 2005–2006 academic year.

Minority Serving Law Schools and Minority Enrollment: There was a significant change in the percentage of minority students who enrolled in the public law schools in Florida following the creation of MSIs (See table 5.9). An examination of the data indicated an increase in the percentage of minority students enrolled at the public law schools. Thus, it was concluded that there was a significant difference in the percentage of minority students enrolled in Florida's public law schools prior to and following the creation of MSIs.

Minority Serving Law Schools and LSAT Scores: Consistent with the findings from question 4b concerning comparison of the mean LSAT scores following implementation of the OFI, a non-significant difference was found in the mean LSAT scores of law school students attending the public law schools prior to and following the creation of MSI law schools, $F(5, 106) = 1.065$, $p > .05$ (See table 5.10). The mean LSAT scores remained relatively unchanged during this period.

## IMPACT OF THE CREATION OF MSI LAW SCHOOLS ON THE DIVERSITY OF FLORIDA'S LEGAL PROFESSION: GRADUATES AND THOSE ADMITTED TO THE BAR

Minority Serving Law Schools and Minority Graduates: There was a non-significant change in the percentage of minority graduates of the public law schools in Florida prior to and following the creation of MSIs (See table 5.11). Thus, Hypothesis 6a was not rejected, and it was concluded that there was not a significant difference in the percentage of minority graduates of Florida's public law schools prior to and following the creation of MSI law schools.

Minority Serving Law Schools and Florida Bar Examination: This hypothesis could not be tested because the FBA indicated that it could not release this information. The data received from the FBA reported the percentage of practicing attorneys who are members of the Florida Bar (See table 5.6).

Some participants believed that creating two MSI law schools would impact diversity in Florida's legal profession over a long-term period by providing increased access to legal education for all Floridians, including minority students. Among those who responded to this question, most said they are not aware of any impact the two MSI law schools have had on diversity in Florida's legal profession. At least one respondent felt that the creation of two MSI law schools coincided with the abandonment of the Minority Participation in Legal Education and Virgil Hawkins Scholarship programs, two financial aid programs intended to increase minority access to a public law school education in Florida.

## IMPLICATIONS OF THE OFI STUDY

This research implies that minorities are at a disadvantage in the legal profession in Florida. The FBA's data supports the fact that there are approximately 1,415 attorneys in Florida's legal profession who were of African American descent and 6,365 who are Hispanic, compared to 62,943 Whites (FBA, 2007). Also, according to data from the Directory of Legal Employers Diversity and Demographics Reports of the NALP (National Association for Law Placement), in 2011, 19.9 percent of associates were minorities, 6.56 percent were partners (Cuyver, 2012). This coincides with other research in both the United States and Europe suggesting that minority lawyers can face difficulties that are sometimes insurmountable while trying to assimilate into the culture of today's legal profession (Marseille, 2016; Roach, 2006). In addition, the legal profession in the United States has been involved for many years in programs it claims are intended to increase minority representation, meeting with only minimal success (Glater, 2001). Minorities are significantly underrepresented in the legal profession, according to Barker (2005), who indicated that Blacks and Hispanics accounted for slightly more than five percent of lawyers in the top 250 grossing law firms in the country. Barker (2010) also noted that the number of Black partners also declined. This trend has shown to be consistent in 2016 according to the American Lawyer, which indicates that, on average, 15 percent of attorneys working in American Law 200 and National Law Journal's 250 firms were minority. While the numbers of Asian-American and Hispanic lawyers at the firms have increased, African-Americans still remain low (McQueen, 2016).

It would appear that the United States is not alone when it comes to harboring an unwelcoming environment for African American lawyers, according to a report published in the British newspaper, *The Independent*. The article claims the lack of young minority lawyers in Britain's leading law firms is somewhat of a self-fulfilling prophecy. The fact that there are so few of them, according to the report, denotes that they are constantly being watched and their work is under continuous scrutiny, creating such pressure on them to perform that many simply collapse and drop out. The report blames the lack of minority lawyers in these firms on the fact that there are insufficient numbers to create role models and a support network ("Lack of Support," 2006). To bolster its claim, the newspaper cites research by Europe's largest minority lawyers' group, the Black Solicitors Network (BSN), showing that there were no ethnic minority partners in one-third of the British law firms surveyed in 2006 by the BSN (Black Solicitors Network, 2006).

Researchers and practitioners have suggested that the lack of minority attorneys has a far-reaching impact that is felt by society as a whole and not just the profession. The ABA (2015) estimates that Blacks make up approximately five percent of America's lawyers, with the result being the underpinnings of distrust of the legal system by racial minorities because they aren't able to find lawyers and judges who look like them (Randall, 2004). The National Bar Association's President, Kim Keenan (2004–2005), goes even further, indicating that as a result of the underrepresentation of African Americans in the law profession, people of color will not be able to find lawyers of color (Mallory, 2005). This is further outlined in Young's (2015) article discussion of the need for Black lawyers, even more so than Black police officers, where interactions between police officers and Black males are resulting in death for Black males. The author suggests that these instances are increasing because of the underrepresentation of Blacks in the courtroom.

The National Association for the Advancement of Colored People (NAACP) recognized the importance of having attorneys who look like the community they are serving to conduct the organization's business. In the early years, the organization was using White lawyers for many of its court fights, but began to face community and political pressure during the 1920's to use Black lawyers. The Black community made it clear that it wanted organizations that worked in the community to represent the community. To an increasing extent, it was not enough that the organization was Black, the community also wanted its representatives, including lawyers, to be Black (Kluger, 1977).

Despite recognition of the importance of diversity in the legal profession of Florida and the nation, the OFI has failed to live up to the promises made by its proponents (Lyons, 2003). Orfield says that his review of the OFI shows that its Talented Twenty plan actually had little impact on qualifying students from high schools who would not ordinarily have qualified prior to implementation of Talented Twenty. Orfield says his research implies that the OFI did not work and its promise of greater diversity was not realized (Lyons, 2003). He says OFI had no impact because most of the state's public universities had no affirmative action policy in the first place, and the Talented Twenty plan did not significantly increase the number of minority students who qualified to attend, for example, UF (Lyons, 2003).

There is an abundance of research to suggest that, with the exception of affirmative action, which the OFI was intended to redefine, few policies promising to bring about greater diversity have been successful (Walker, 2007). Further, Rhode (2015) suggests that law is the least diverse profession in the nation and little is being done to rectify these disparities. Far from being a panacea, however, it appears affirmative action alone does not guarantee equal treatment for minorities in the hiring and promotion process.

There is evidence suggesting that, even with affirmative action, minorities face obstacles that are difficult to overcome. In the federal government, for example, opportunities for minorities are declining in areas one might not expect, as shown in a recent television news investigative report by WJLA-TV in Washington, DC.

> Since 2003, the criminal section within the Civil Rights Division has not hired a single Black attorney to replace those who have left. Not one. As a result, the current face of civil rights prosecutions looks like this: Out of fifty attorneys in the Criminal Section, only two are Black. The same number the criminal section had in 1978, even though the size of the staff has more than doubled (Baskin, 2007).

According to the television report, the Justice Department responded by pointing out that the Civil Rights Division is more diverse than any other in the Department of Justice.

## IMPACT OF THE OFI STUDY

Why are states such as Florida moving further away from the customary use of affirmative action policies and towards the OFI and initiatives like it? That is not a question that this study was prepared to answer. Ward Connerly may be the best person to provide the answer to that question. He is chairman of the American Civil Rights Institute and was actively involved in initiatives to reduce the use of affirmative action in California, Washington State, and Michigan. Connerly believes affirmative action sends the wrong message for the nation. In an interview with *The Chronicle of Higher Education*, he said his goal is to get America to apply one standard to every citizen, regardless of race (Schmidt, 2007).

Ward Connerly believes affirmative action amounts to privileging some citizens over others, and he pushed to get more states to abandon their affirmative action policies. He assisted with ballot initiatives in Arizona, Colorado, Missouri, and Oklahoma in time for the Presidential Election in November 2008 (Antonio & Muniz, 2007; Ryman & Benson, 2007). In addition, Connerly suggested that more states would follow. He predicted that either Nebraska or South Dakota would be the next state to abandon affirmative action (Schmidt, 2007). The state of Nebraska took similar action in 2008, while others such as Colorado, Arizona, Oklahoma, and Missouri were considering anti-affirmative action legislation (Ryman & Benson, 2007; Antonio & Muniz, 2007). More recently, a total of eight states have banned race-based affirmative action at all public universities, including California, Washington, Michigan, Nebraska, Arizona, Connecticut, Oklahoma, and New Hampshire (Potter, 2014).

Who benefits from states abandoning affirmative action policies? The answer to that question may surprise those who would expect that White applicants would be the primary beneficiaries. More specifically, White women are cited as the primary beneficiary from affirmative action, although they are among those who fight against it the most. The evidence resulted from the *Fisher v. Texas* in which the Supreme Court upheld affirmative action after a White woman sought to undo it due to her belief that her chance at admission was due to her race (Angyal, 2016).

> Eliminating affirmative action would reduce acceptance rates for African American and Hispanic applicants by as much as one-half to two-thirds and have an equivalent impact on the proportion of underrepresented minority students in the admitted class. White applicants would benefit very little by removing racial and ethnic preferences; the White acceptance rate would increase by roughly 0.5 percentage point. Asian applicants would gain the most. They would occupy four out of every five seats created by accepting fewer African American and Hispanic students. (Espenshade & Chung, 2005 303–304).

Some researchers believe that affirmative action actually inhibits minorities. They point to research suggesting that without affirmative action, there would be more minorities in law school and in the practice of law. Such is the case involving a study by Richard Sander (2004), whose research claimed that African Americans would be better off without affirmative action. In Sander's study, he claims that African Americans perform significantly worse in law school than their White counterparts and that affirmative action only sets up most of them for eventual failure (Sander, 2004).

Among those who have added their voice to the chorus of people questioning the effects and effectiveness of affirmative action is the United States Commission on Civil Rights. The group recently released a report that appears to take sides in the debate over affirmative action in law schools. In the report, the commission calls on national and state leaders to force law schools to release information detailing how and under what circumstances they employ affirmative action policies in their admission decisions and the success rate of minority students who enroll (Schmidt, 2007). The Commission also calls on the law school accreditation arm of the ABA to abandon its rule that requires law schools seeking accreditation to prove that they are committed to diversity.

It is a controversial report that has those on both sides of the affirmative action debate taking sides, even among those who are commission members. The eight-member panel was divided in its decision to release the report (Schmidt, 2007). Opponents believe it will be used by researchers like Richard Sander, the University of California at Los Angeles law professor whose 2004 study is the subject of great controversy. Sander believes that Blacks do poorly in law school and have a lower bar passage rate than Whites because they were admitted under affirmative action, and not by their merit.

Some researchers, including Harris and Kidder (2005), dispute Sander's study. After analyzing his data, they reach different conclusions. Their research shows that Blacks are performing below their White counterparts in law school, as Sander claimed, but the difference, they found, is not significant. They also predicted that rather than being better off without affirmative action with an increase of eight percent in law school admissions, the number of Blacks in law school would actually have declined significantly in 2004 if there had been no affirmative action (Harris & Kidder, 2005).

## RECOMMENDATIONS

Based on the findings of the study, recommendations were made in the areas of policy, practice, and further research. Each of these areas is discussed below.

### Policy

The authors assume that affirmative action is also of benefit to increasing diversity in all graduate and professional schools. It is apparently not the only policy that has proven effective in diversifying America's law schools and the practice of law. The recommendation to communities around the country, as a result of this study, is to resist the temptation to pass legislation that might have the effect of inhibiting the growth of diversity. It seems as if communities may want to consider more carefully the impact of such policies because of the possibility of further damaging minority growth in higher education, damage that could take years to repair.

### Practice

This study suggests, but does not prove, the kinds of results that might be expected with implementation of laws and policies similar to the OFI in other states. The limitations of this study prevent expanding its results to other states; however, it does call into question whether similar results might be anticipated. For this reason, and because several states are considering initiatives similar to the OFI, the authors recommend further research into the impact of policies that are intended to redefine affirmative action in other states. Even more intriguing is the likelihood of determining what effects these policies might produce with respect to minority access to higher education in these states. Given what we have seen in this study, it is anticipated that such policies implemented in other states would yield similar results—minorities gaining improved access to specialized graduate and professional programs offered in higher education institutions, despite an overall disadvantage.

## Further Research

While this study examined the impact of the OFI in Florida, from the perspectives of law school deans and admissions personnel, the authors believe that further study is warranted in this area. For example, data that measures perceptions of law school students in the academy and those who are in the legal profession would add considerably to the wealth of knowledge about this issue. One might also consider replicating this study in the future to include data gathered from private law schools in the state of Florida. Law schools whose administrators' perceptions have not been studied include: St. Thomas University, University of Miami, Stetson University, Barry University, Nova Southeastern University Shepard Broad Law Center, and Florida Coastal School of Law. This study may also be replicated in other specialized fields where minorities are underrepresented, such as science, engineering, and others. Furthermore, it is conceivable that this study be expanded to other states, such as Texas, California, Washington, and Michigan, where similar initiatives or proposals have been implemented to redefine affirmative action. The results of those studies can then be compared with the results from this research in Florida to determine if there are any similarities of outcomes.

From the perspective of a critical race theorist, this research might have examined the tenets of CRT as they relate to the implementation of the OFI and opening two MSI law schools with the intersection of race, gender, and class. This study, however, did not examine the intersection of race, gender, and class. It may be that one should consider examining the use of gender and class in determining the impact of the OFI and the addition of two MSI law schools on the legal education landscape of Florida. A critical race theorist, for example, may seek to analyze whether creating two MSI law schools might advance a separatist position as well as encourage Black Nationalist beliefs. Such is not the conclusion of this study; however, further research into this area is appropriate.

When any new policy is implemented, it requires and deserves the scrutiny of researchers who will spend years analyzing the impact of such policy changes to determine if the actual results bear any resemblance to that which was promised or intended. Additional studies on this subject would serve the interests of higher education and the underrepresented in America. If it is found that policies intended to redefine affirmative action are harming the pursuit of diversity, it then serves the public interest to learn as much about the topic area as possible.

## SUMMARY

This study and the results it produced can be used to assist lawmakers, policy makers, higher education administrators, and others to gain a better understanding of the impact of policies that seek to enhance diversity at the local, state, and national levels. Citizens and legislatures in states that may be considering introducing or passing laws that redefine affirmative action are strongly urged to review and examine this study very closely. An analysis of this research can be helpful in anticipating the results that might be expected from any efforts to legislate changes to affirmative action policies. Likewise, individuals who are advocates for policies that seek to encourage greater diversity will find this study of assistance to them when asking their communities to make informed decisions.

In conclusion, this study found the representation of minorities in Florida's legal profession improved after implementation of OFI and the addition of two MSI law schools. In addition, this study concluded that minorities were represented in larger numbers in Florida SUS law schools; however, Black representation among students in law schools in the SUS of Florida as well as around the country has failed to make strides that either affirmative action or race neutral incentives have promised.

Data from the SUS of Florida public law schools suggest admission and enrollment numbers that rank Whites in first place, well ahead of other ethnic groups, Hispanic students second, Blacks in third place, and Asian Americans and Native Americans fourth. These numbers are not unlike those that are certified by the FBA for the current percentage of attorneys by race. As critical race theorists, the authors believe that while the intent of the OFI and the creation of two MSI law schools was to improve diversity, Whites benefited most because their opportunities to attend law schools in the SUS of Florida were expanded.

Black law school enrollment was actually better nationally prior to implementation of various initiatives in states around the country that reduced their use of traditional affirmative action policies. For example, the nation's ABA-accredited law schools boasted an enrollment of 7.1 percent Black in 2000 and only 6.2 percent in the 2005–2006 academic year ("Black Student," 2007). An article entitled, "Black student enrollments in law school inch higher," indicated that the number of Blacks in law schools is increasing, albeit slowly, with a 3.6 percent rise in total enrollment or 9,529 Black students in 2006–2007 ("Black Student," 2007).

By the weight of evidence widely available, one can only conclude that minorities continue to be vastly underrepresented in colleges of law and, by extension, in the legal profession. The plight of minorities in law school has evolved despite improvements brought about by the use of affirmative action and race conscious practices meant to enhance minority enrollment. It is apparent that opening the two MSI law schools in Florida did not encourage the predominately White law schools to withdraw their traditional support of minorities in gaining admittance to their programs.

While it would be irresponsible for the authors to try and predict what the future holds, the situation represents numerous opportunities for further research into such complex issues as: What impact will Florida's decision to abandon all but race neutral policies in its admissions practices in public law schools have on the private law institutions? What is the actual long-term effect of Florida's implementation of the OFI on the state's minority law population? How can there be middle ground found between two such widely disparate points of view? And, what are the long-term implications for the minority population of states who do not have an adequate number of minority lawyers to satisfy the perceived need of the minority community? Clearly, there is a need for additional research in this area and hopefully this study will lead to future discussion on this subject matter.

# Epilogue

## THE STUDY OF THE PERCEPTIONS OF ADMINISTRATORS CONCERNING THE ONE FLORIDA INITIATIVE

The foregoing study examined an exceedingly complex socioeconomic and political dimension of the larger society but, in particular, the narrower legal education process and access for underrepresented minorities in higher education. Moreover, this study centered on exploring access to the four public law schools in the state of Florida, contextualized by a gubernatorial executive order. Although focused on the perceptions of law school administrators regarding the impact of Governor Jeb Bush's One Florida Initiative (OFI) (Executive Order 99-281, 1999) on minority access, admission, and completion of Florida's four public law schools, it presents not only the need for further qualitative and quantitative research on the effect of OFI and other such legislative initiatives, but also provides a basis for a more substantive examination/consideration of the foundational premises of the "promise" and the "product" of such legislative acts. This study lays a foundation for deeper critical examination and analysis of the fundamental basis for legislative acts that seemingly refute the racial basis for legal discrimination in the first place, by actively calling for race-neutral decisions/contexts that afford persons access to economic, political, and social aspects of the larger society. This juxtaposition poses a serious conflict for the effective resolution of the problem.

In this regard it is important, however, to keep in mind an essential balance to be considered, as in most things, between the "promise" and the "product" of legislation such as the One Florida Initiative. On one hand the "promise" is that OFI would over time provide for increased underrepresented minority participation in the legal professions and other business ventures in the state.

It was executed as the vehicle for redefining affirmative action, changing/increasing access, and ultimately providing the opportunity for participants/beneficiaries to improve their status as contractors, professionals, as lawyers. OFI sought to redefine affirmative action without the use of race. Its intent was "to amalgamate Floridians with a shared vision and to increase opportunities and diversity in the State University System where the use of race is not permissible." According to Governor Jeb Bush, "The OFI is diversity without quotas, preferences, or set-asides and it was designated not to abandon affirmative action, but to substantially redefine it" (Bush 2000, p.1).

The argument of OFI lacks apparent/seeming recognition of the sensitivity or awareness necessary within and for those who would make such decisions about college admissions or contracting. Or perhaps, it is a maladroit conclusion that the sensitivity/awareness is inherently present in those who make decisions about admission, acceptance, and successful passage of the Florida Bar by virtue of their history and experience. It raises the question of whether one can, by the stroke of a pen, abandon the racial basis upon which government, social structures, and institutions were established in the state and the country. It seems in this "promise" to have avoided/ignored criteria for how this "amalgamation" might effectively be achieved for segments of the citizens in Florida who have historically been denied or had restricted access to any education, let alone legal education, without some additional guidance and tools for bringing about changes in the people who make the decisions and perpetuate their control over the decisions.

In considering the "product" of this "promise"—increased access, completion, success, and enjoyment of the benefits of economic prosperity—long denied, will those who block and control such entry, relinquish or rather, *allow* minimal parceling of such? What this study offers, among many things too numerous to mention here, is that more incisive probing is required with a view toward addressing the values, attitudes, and habits of those who seek to maintain control.

John T. Wolfe, Jr.
Founder & CEO—Avant-Garde Educational Services

# Reflections

When I conceived of this study, it was something that I believed in and thought I would enjoy pursuing. The subject matter is one in which I have been deeply interested for several years. I have been curious for some time about the effectiveness of the OFI and the impact of opening two MSI law schools on increasing diversity in Florida's public law schools. In doing the study, however, I found it to be much more difficult than I expected.

Initially, I was disappointed to find that adequate data on the subject was not as available as I thought. I found there to be a lack of information to assist me in developing the study, which caused me to exert more time and effort toward discovering data necessary for this research. It was, for example, difficult to obtain mission statements for each school dating back to pre-OFI years, in order to compare them with present day mission statements.

There were other obstacles that I needed to overcome in order to complete this study. The obvious and most anticipated problem was a result of attempting to do research over an extended distance. Achieving simple communication with individuals to participate in the study proved to be a challenge. Also, given the nature of the positions of those I had to interview for my research, namely law school deans and admissions personnel, I found everyone's schedules to be extremely busy. This resulted in difficulty trying to arrange time for face-to-face interviews, and in some cases, convincing these administrators to find the time on their schedules to respond to an interview questionnaire. In addition, there was a change in leadership at FAMU at about the same time I was attempting to do my research. The leadership change created uncertainty and, to some degree, problems for me when contacting the appropriate individuals to participate in the study. It was, perhaps, the use of human subjects that presented the most interesting challenge. I had to overcome some reluctance by participants to take part in the study. Some of the reluctance I encountered, I believe, can be attributed to the sensitive nature of the subject matter. It is often considered human nature for people to exhibit reluctance to openly discuss issues related to race, sex, religion, and other sensitive topics. Such is the potential weakness of any study that involves issues considered to be sensitive when one is relying on qualitative methods using human subjects.

# References

*Adarand Constructors v. Pena*, 515 U.S. 200 (1995).

Aday, J.C. (2011). Fitting square pegs into round holes: How race-based affirmative action in higher education admissions is an inadequate and inequitable means to an end. *University of Massachusetts Law Review 6*(1), 125–57. Retrieved 13 July 2015 from http://scholarship.law.umassd.edu/umlr/vol6/iss1/6.

African-American students at historically Black law schools. (2007). Journal *of Blacks in Higher Education*. Retrieved September 13, 2007, from http://www.jbhe.com/latest/index091307.html.

Aguirre, A. (2000). Academic storytelling: A critical race theory story of affirmative action. *Sociological Perspectives* (*43*)2, 319–39. doi: 10.2307/1389799.

Alabama State Constitution. Code of Alabama (1901).

Alder, P.A., & Alder, P. (1987). Membership roles in field research. Newbury Park, CA: Sage Publications.

Alfiery, A., & Onwuachi-Willig,A. (2013) Next-Generation civil rights lawyers: Race and representation in the age of identity performance. *Yale Law Journal 122*, 1484–558.

Allen, W.R., & Jewel, J.O. (2002). A backward glance forward: Past, present, future perspectives on historically Black colleges and universities. *The Review of Higher Education*, 25(3), 241–261.

American Bar Association (2006). Enrollment data report.

American Bar Association (2012). "Racial and ethnic diversity in the American Bar Association." Retrieved from http://www.americanbar.org/content/dam/aba/administrative/racial_ethnic_diversity/REG3Rpt12_finalweb_updated3_13_12.authcheckdam.pdf.

American Indian College Fund. (2014). *TCU timeline.* Retrieved from http://www.collegefund.org/content/tcu_timeline.

Among the nation's 30 top-rated law schools, Harvard has the highest percentage of Black students. (2007). *Journal of Blacks in Higher Education*. Retrieved from http://www.jbhe.com/latest/index090607.html.

Association of American Colleges and Universities. (1995). *The drama of diversity and democracy: Higher education and American commitments.* Washington, DC: AAC&U.

Associated Press (2004, June 19). Appeals court dismisses NAACP's One Florida lawsuit. St. Petersberg Times. Retrieved from http://www.sptimes.com/2004/06/19/State/Appeals_court_dismiss.shtml.

Associated Press (1988, February 15). Virgil D. Hawkins; Broke color barrier to become lawyer. New York Times. Retrieved from http://www.nytimes.com/1988/02/15/obituaries/virgil-d-hawkins-broke-color-barrier-to-become-lawyer.html.

Baker, G.A. III. (1994). A handbook on the community college in America: Its history, mission, and management. Westport, CT: Greenwood Press.

Ballotpedia (n.d.). California Affirmative Action, Prop 209 (1996). Retrieved from http://ballotpedia.org/California_Affirmative_Action,_Proposition_209_(1996).

Baskin, R. (2007, May 4). Only two Black attorneys in Department of Justice Civil Rights Division. Retrieved July 12, 2007, from http://thinkprogress.org/2007/05/07/only-two-black-attorneys-in-dojs-civil-rights-division/.

Bernstein, A. (2002, May 20). Too many workers? Not for long. *Business Week, 126–130.*

Bernstein, R. (2005). Florida, California and Texas to dominate future population growth, census bureau reports. U.S. Census Bureau News. Retrieved November 13, 2006, from http://www.census.gov/Press-Release/www/releases/archives/population/004704.html.

*Biondi v. City of Chicago*, 303 F3d 765 (2002).

Blacks percentage of students at state universities in Florida continues to slide. (2006). *Journal of Blacks in Higher Education.* Retrieved September 28, 2006, from http://www.jbhe.com/latest/index092806_p.html.

Black student enrollments in law school inch higher. (2007). *Journal of Blacks in Higher Education.* Retrieved August 30, 2007, from http://www.jbhe.com/latest/index083007_p.html.

Black Solicitors Network. (2006). The diversity league table. (London: England).

Bowen, W.G., & Rudenstein, N.L. (2002). *In pursuit of the Ph.D.* Princeton, NJ. Princeton University Press.

*Brown v. Board of Education*, 347 U.S. 483 (1954).

*Brown v. Board of Education* (II), 349 U.S. 294 (1955).

Brown, C. M., II. (2001). Collegiate desegregation and the public Black college: A new policy mandate. *The Journal of Higher Education, 72*(1), 46–62.

Brown, C. M., II. Donahoo, S., & Bertrando, R.D. (2001). The Black college and the quest for educational opportunity. *Urban Education 36*(5), 533–571.

Brown, H.B. (1896). *Plessy v. Ferguson* majority opinion. U.S. Supreme Court.

Burger, W. (1972). Griggs *v. Duke Power Co.* majority opinion. U.S. Supreme Court.

Bush, G. (2003). Says affirmative action unconstitutional, Retrieved March 20, 2005, from www.capitolhillblue.com.

Bush, J. (2000). One Florida yields big gains in minority enrollment. Tallahassee, FL. Office of the Governor. Retrieved March 26, 2006, from http://www.oneflorida.org/myflorida/government/governorinitiatives/one_florida/statementForward.html.

Callan, P.M., & Finney, J.E. (2002). Assessing educational capital: An imperative for policy. *Change*, *34* (4).

Callaway, R. (1979). Teachers beliefs concerning values and the functions and purpose of schooling, *Eric Document Reproduction Service*, No. ED 177110.

Calmore, J. (1993). Spatial equality and the kerner commission report: A back to the future essay. *North Carolina Law Review*, *78*, 1487–1518.

Carnevale, A. P., & Desrochers, D.M. (2003). *Standards for what? The economic roots of k–16 reform*. Princeton, NJ: Educational Testing Service.

*City of Richmond v. J.A. Croson Co*., 488 U.S. 469 (1989).

*Civil Rights Act*. Pub. L. 88–352. (1964).

Chambliss, E. (2004). *Miles to go*: *Progress of minorities in the legal profession*. Retrieved January 23, 2007, from www.abanet.org/minorities.

Clark, B.R. (1983). *The Higher Education System.* Berkeley: University of California Press.

Clinton, W. (1994). Educational excellence for Hispanic Americans. Executive Order 12900.

Cohen, A. (1998). *The shaping of American higher education.* San Francisco, CA: Jossey-Bass Publishers.

Connor, L. (1985). *The impact of affirmative action on the employment practices in Pennsylvania's state system of higher education, 1974–1984.* Unpublished doctoral dissertation, University of Pittsburgh.

Conway, M. (2000). Political participation in United States. *Congressional Quarterly, Inc.*

Connerly, W. (2007). It is time to end race-based 'Affirmative Action'." *Univ. Of St. Thomas Journal Of Law & Public Policy* 1.1, 56–62.

Cooper, F. (2002). The un-balanced fourth amendment: A cultural study of the drug war, racial profiling and arvizu. *Villanova Law Review*, *47*, 851–895.

Crenshaw, K.W. (2011). Twenty years of critical race theory: Looking back to move forward. *Connecticut Law Review*, *43*(5),1253–352.

Crenshaw, K.W. (2002). The first decade: Critical reflections, or a foot in the closing door. *UCLA Law Review*, *49*, 1343–1372.

Crenshaw, K.W. (1988): Race, reform, and retrenchment: Transformation and legitimation in antidiscrimination law. *Harvard Law Review* *101*(7),1331–1387. doi:10.2307/1341398.

Crenshaw, K., Gotanda, N., Peller, G., & Thomas, K. (Eds.). (1995). *Critical race theory*. New York: The New Press.

Creswell, J. (1994). *Research design*: *Qualitative and quantitative approaches*. Newbury Park, CA: Sage Publications.

Crum, S. (1989). The history of Tribal Colleges. *Tribal College Journal*, *1*, 1.

Davenport, W. (1991). Development of a survey of faculty attitudes to determine the need for a faculty development plan in affirmative action at Broome Community College. New York: Nova University. (Eric Document Reproduction Service No. ED 3404341).

Davidson, R.C., & Lewis, E.L. (1997). Affirmative action and other special consideration admissions at the University of California Davis, School of Medicine. *Journal of the American Medical Association*, *278*, 1153–1158.

de Gruyter, W. (1992). *American Universities and Colleges, 14th ed.*

Daye, C.E., Panter, A.T., Allen, W.R. & Wightman, L.F. (2012, August 1). Does race matter in educational diversity? A legal and empirical analysis. *Rutgers Race and the Law Review*. Forthcoming. Retrieved from http://ssrn.com/abstract=2101253.

Delgado, R. (1995). Affirmative action as a majoritarian device: Or, do you really want to be a role model? In R. Delgado (Ed.), CRT: The cutting edge. Philadelphia: Temple University Press.

Delgado, R. and Stefancic,J. (2001). *Critical race theory: An introduction*. New York: New York University Press.

Delgado, R. and Stefancic, J. (1995). *Critical Race Theory, An Annotated Bibliography*. "1993: A Year of Transition" *University of Colorado Law Review 66*, 159–193.

Denzin, N., & Lincoln, Y. (1994). *Handbook of qualitative research*. Thousand Oaks, CA: Sage Publications.

Dickinson, E. (2012) Addressing justice narrative framework. *Communication, Culture & Critique* 5, 57–74.

Dougherty, K.J. (1994). *The contradictory college*: *The conflicting origins, impacts, and futures of the community college*. Albany, NY: State University of New York Press. \

Ellis, P. (2006). *Law career access*: *An examination of the occupational outcomes for University of Maryland School of Law graduates (Class of 2000–2003).* Unpublished doctoral dissertation, Morgan State University.

Elwell, F. (2002). The sociology of C. Wright Mills. Retrieved November 20, 2005, from http://www.faculty.rsu.edu/~felwell/Theorists/Mills/index.htm.

Espenshade, T.J., & Chung, C.Y. (2005). The opportunity cost of admission preferences at elite universities. *Social Science Quarterly*; *86*(293), 303–304.

Ewell, P.T. (1999). Assessment of higher education and quality: Promise and politics. In S.J. Messick (Ed.), *Assessment in higher education*: *Issues of access, quality, student development, and public policy*. Mahwah, NJ: Erlbaum.

Executive Order 13096 (2002). Navajo Nation.

Executive Order 11246 (1965).

Executive Order 11748 (1969).

Executive Order 99–281 (1999). Retrieved from http://www.dms.myflorida.com/content/download/705/3389/file/ExecutiveOrder99–281.pdf.

Fisher, W.R. (1985). The narrative paradigm: An elaboration. *Communication Monographs*, *52*, 347–367.

*Fisher v. University of Texas at Austin*, 758 F.3d 633 (5th Cir. 2014).

Fleming, J. (1976). *The lengthening shadow of slavery*: *A historical justification for affirmative action for Blacks in higher education*. Washington, DC: Howard University Press.

Fleming, J., Gill, G., & Swinton, D. H. (1978). *The case for affirmative action for Blacks in higher education*. Washington, DC: Institute for the Study of Educational Policy, Howard University Press.

Florida Department of Education. (2013). The fact book. Report for the Florida college system. Retrieved December 8, 2014 from http://www.fldoehub.org/CCTCMIS/c/Documents/Fact%20Books/fb2013.pdf.

Florida Department of Management Systems (1999). *State contracts and agreements. Executive order 99–281*. Retrieved from http://www.dms.myflorida.com/content/download/705/3389/file/ExecutiveOrder99–281.pdf.

Florida Education Fund (n.d.). MPLE Program. Retrieved from http://fefonline.org/mple.html.

Florida Postsecondary Education Planning Commission (1999, December). Minority participation in Legal Education Program. Retrieved from http://www.cepri.state.fl.us/Documents/ProjectsIndexedBy/mplefin.pdf.

Florida Statutes Chapter 240.7105, 2001

Florida Statutes Chapter 240.7101, 2001

Freeman, K. (2005). *African Americans in college choice: The influence of family and school*. New York: State University of New York.

Frye, J.H. (1992). *The vision of the public junior college, 1900–1940*. Westport, CT: Greenwood Press.

Gannon, M. (1996). The *New History of Florida*. Gainesville: Florida. University of Florida Press.

Garibaldi, A. (1991). *The role of historically Black colleges in facilitating resilience among African American students. Education and Urban Society, 24, 103–112.*

Gasman, M. (2009). Minority-serving colleges deserve more respect. The Chronicle of Higher Education, Retrieved from http://search.proquest.com/docview/214656251?accountid=13758.

Gillborn, D. (2009). Who's afraid of critical race theory in education? A reply to Mike Cole's "The Color-Line and the Class Struggle." *Power and Education 1*,1125–131. doi: 10.2304/power.2009.1.1.125.

Goldman, A. (1979). *Justice and reverse discrimination*. Princeton, NJ: Princeton University Press.

*Gratz v. Bollinger*, 539 U.S. 244 (2003).

*Griggs v. Duke Power Co*., 401 U.S. 424 (1971).

*Grutter v. Bollinger*, 539 U.S. 306 (2003).

Hamel, J., Dufour, S., & Fortin, D. (1993). *Case study methods*. Newbury Park, CA: Sage Publications.

Harris, C. (2002). Critical race studies. *UCLA Law Review*, *49*, 1215–1240.

Harris, C.I., & Kidder, W.C. (2005). The Black student mismatch myth in legal education: The systemic flaws in Richard Sander's affirmative action study. *The Journal of Blacks in Higher Education*, *46*, 102–105.

*Hawkins v. Board of Control*, 350 U.S. 413 (1950).

Herbert, A.W. (1999). Remarks and recommendations regarding additional law schools. Florida Board of Regents meeting, Tallahassee, FL.

Henderson, Nia-Malida. The Washington Post. Jeb Bush did really well with Latinos in Florida. It probably doesn't mean much for 2016. December 15, 2014. Retrieved from http://www.washingtonpost.com/blogs/the-fix/wp/2014/12/15/jeb-bush-did-really-well-with-latinos-in-florida-it-probably-doesnt-mean-much-for-2016/.

Hinrichs, P. (2012) The effects of affirmative action bans on college enrollment, educational attainment, and the demographic composition of universities. *The Review of Economics and Statistics 94*(3), 712–22.

Hispanic Association of Colleges and Universities. (2014). Hispanic serving institution definitions. Retrieved from http://www.hacu.net/hacu/HSI_Definition.asp.

*Hopwood v. State of Texas*, 78 F. 3d 932 (5th Cir.) 1996.

Howard University. (2006). *History of Howard University School of Law*. Retrieved March 20, 2007, from http://www.law.howard.edu/19.

Humes, Karen R., Jones, Nicolas A., and Ramirez, Roberto R (2011). "Overview of Race and Hispanic Origin: 2010." U.S. Census Bureau.

Hutchinson, D. (1999). Ignoring the sexualization of race: Heteronormativity, critical race theory, and anti-racist politics. *Buffalo Law Review*, *47*, 1–116.

Jed Bush's One Florida plan continues to damage Black enrollments at the state's most prestigious law schools. (2006). *Journal of Blacks in Higher Education*. Retrieved March 29, 2007 from http://www.jbhe.com/latest/index042006.html.

Johnson, L.B. (1969). Executive Order 11748.

Johnson, L.B. (1965). Executive Order 11246.

Katsinas, S.G., & Opp, R.D. (2001). *Title III: A critically important federal initiative supporting rural community colleges. MDC, Inc. Chapel Hill, NC, Retrieved January 20, 2007, from www.mdcinc.org/rcc/titleiii.pdf.*

Kahlenberg, R.D., Ed. (2014*). The future of affirmative action: New paths to higher education diversity after* Fisher v. University of Texas. 1st Ed. New York: Century Foundation.

[Kathryn]. (2014, June 25). Virgil Hawkins and the fight to integrate University of Florida Law School. [blog post]. Retrieved from https://www.floridamemory.com/blog/2014/06/25/virgil062514/.

King, M.L. (1963, April 16). Letter from a Birmingham jail. African Studies Center—University of Pennsylvania. Retrieved from https://www.africa.upenn.edu/Articles_Gen/Letter_Birmingham.html.

Klink, M. (2003). *The reestablishment of the Florida Agricultural and Mechanical University College of Law: A policy analysis of equality of educational opportunity and legal education policy making in Florida (1949–2000)*. Unpublished doctoral dissertation, The Florida State University.

Kluger, R. (1977). *Simple justice: The history of Brown v. Board of Education and Black America's struggle for equality.* New York: Vintage Books.

Lack of support. (2006, April 6). Lack of support leads to young Black lawyers struggling to survive. *The Independent.* Retrieved June 20, 2007, from http://education.independent.co.uk/careers_advice/article355931.ece.

Ladson-Billings, G., & Tate IV, W. (1995). Toward a critical race theory of education." *Teachers College Record,* 979(1), 47–68.

Ladson-Billings, G. (1998) Just what is critical race theory and what's it doing in a nice field like education. *International Journal of Qualitative Studies in Education 11*(1),7–24.

Laurent, A. (1999) What is affirmative action? *Government Executive.* Retrieved March 20, 2005, from www.govexec.com.

Legal Information Institute. The State of Florida Ex. Rel. Virgil D. Hawkins, Petitioner v. The Board of Control, et al. Retrieved from https://www.law.cornell.edu/supremecourt/text/350/413.

Liptak, A. (2015, June 29). Supreme Court to weigh race in college admissions. *The New York Times.* p.A1.

Louisiana State Constitution. Louisiana Acts No. 111, p. 152. (1890).

Lovett, B.L. (1990). Black adult education during the Civil War, 1861–1865. In H.G. Neufeldt, & L. McGee. (Eds.). *Education of the African American adult: An historical overview.* New York: Greenwood Press.

Lyons, D. (2003). Gary Orfield on One Florida. *South Florida Sun-Sentinel.* Retrieved June 23, 2007, from http://www.racematters.org/garyorfieldononeflorida.htm.

Mallory, K. (2005 August 5). Black presence in law schools dwindling. *The Chicago Defender.*

Marin, P., & Lee, E. (2003). Appearance and reality in the sunshine state: The talented 20 program in Florida. Retrieved, April 20, 2007, from http://www.civilrightsproject.harvard.edu/research/affirmativeaction/tristate.php.

McCormick, J.L. (1972). The role of the federal government in student financial aid: A history. *The Journal of Student Financial Aid, 2*, p. 47.

McDonough, P., Antonio A.L., & Trent, J.W. (1997). *Black students, Black colleges: An African American college choice model. Journal for a Just and Caring Society, 3*, 9–36.

*McLaurin v. Board of Regents of Oklahoma*, 339 U.S. 637 (1950).

McPhail, I.P. (2005). Top 10 reasons to attend a community college. *Community College Week, 17*, 11: 4–5.

Merriam, S. (1998). *Qualitative research and case study applications in education.* San Francisco, CA: Jossey-Bass Publications.

Michigan Civil Rights Committee. (2006). What is the Michigan civil rights initiative? Retrieved January 20, 2007, from http://www.michigancivilrights.org/media/MCRI_FAQs.pdf.

Milakovich, M., & Gordon, G. (2001). *Public administration in America* (7th ed.). Belmont, CA: Wadworth Group Thomson Learning.

Mills, Charles W. (1997). *The Racial Contract.* Ithaca: Cornell UP.

Mingers, J., & Brocklesby, J. (1997). Multimethodology: Towards a framework for mixing methodologies. *Omega*, 25(5), 489–509.

Moore, J. (2000). Florida students organize to defend affirmative action from Connerly, Gov. Jeb Bush. *Motion Magazine*. Retrieved January 20, 2007, from http://www.inmotionmagazine.com/jm.html.

National Center for Higher Education Management Systems. (1993). *Increasing minority participation in The Florida Bar: An analysis of current legal education conditions and options.* Boulder, Co: Young Lawyers Division of The Florida Bar.

Nettles, M. T., & Millett, C.M. (2006). *Three magic letters; Getting to Ph.D.* Johns Hopkins University Press.

Neyland, L.W. (2000). *The rise, fall and rebirth of the Florida A&M University College of Law*. Tallahassee: Florida A&M University Press.

Neyland, L.W. (2001) *Florida Agricultural and Mechanical University: Sixteen years of excellence with caring (1985–2001).* Tallahassee, FL: Florida A&M University Foundation.

North Carolina Central University. (2007). *History of North Carolina Central University School of Law*. Retrieved March 26, 2007, from http://web.nccu.edu/law/about/history.html.

O'Connor, S.D. (2003). *Grutter v. Bollinger* majority opinion. U.S. Supreme Court.

Office of the Governor. (1999). One Florida Initiative, Executive Order No. 99–281.

Orfield, G., & Miller, E. (1998). *Chilling admissions: The affirmative action crisis and the search for alternatives.* Civil Rights Project, Harvard University Press.

Paget-Clark, N. (1999). Ward Connerly is bringing his anti-affirmative action campaign to Florida. *Motion Magazine*. Retrieved January 20, 2007 from http://www.inmotionmagazine.com/cbrown.html.

Penner, D.S. (1998). The heritage of university planning: *Medieval colleges: Early development of universities*. Berkshire, England: Newbold College Press.

Pérez Huber, L, & Solorzano, D.G. "Racial Microaggressions as a tool for critical race research." *Race Ethnicity and Education* (2014): 297–320, 13 July 2015. Retrieved from http://dx.doi.org/10.1080/13613324.2014.994173.

*Plessy v. Ferguson*, 163 U.S. 537 (1896).

Powell, J. (1978). *University of California Regents v. Bakke* majority opinion. United States Supreme Court.

Proposition 209 Analysis. (1996). Retrieved March 26, 2006, from http://vote96.ss.ca.gov/Vote96/html/BP/209.htm.

Raise Black enrollment by dropping One Florida. (2006, September 18). *Palm Beach Post*.

Randall, V. (2004). The 2004 Whitest law schools report. Retrieved January 23, 2007, from http://academic.udayton.edu/race/03justice/LegalEd/Whitest/index.htm.

Rashdall, H. (1936). *The universities of Europe in the Middle Ages*. England: Oxford University, Clarendon Press.

Reskin, B.F. (1998). *The realities of affirmative action in an employment*. Washington, DC: American Sociological Association.

*Ritchie, D. A. (2003). Doing Oral History: A Practical Guide. Oxford University Press.*

*Rivers, L.O. (2000). Florida A&M University College of Law (1949–2000). Tallahassee, FL: Florida A&M University Press.*

Roach, R. (2006). Getting to the truth. Diverse Issues in Higher Education, *23*(21), 24–28.

Roebuck, J. and Murty, K. (1993). *Historically Black colleges and universities: Their place in American higher education*. Wesport, CT: Praefer.

Sander, R.H. (2004). A systemic analysis of affirmative action in American law schools. *Stanford Law Review*, *57*, 367.

Schmidt, P. (2007). 4 states named as new targets in affirmative action fight. The Chronicle of Higher Education, *53*(35), A34–A35.

Schmidt, P. (2007). Civil-Rights panel wants law schools required to disclose key affirmative-action data. *The Chronicle of Higher Education*. Retrieved August 28, 2007, from http://chronicle.com/daily/2007/08/2007082801n.htm.

Schuster, K. (2000, February 18). Regents approve One Florida plan. *Sun Sentinel.* Retrieved from http://articles.sun-sentinel.com/2000–02–18/news/0002180223_1_new-admissions-admissions-rules-preferences.

*Senate Bill 68. (2002). Tallahassee, FL: The Florida Senate.*

*Senate Bill 140. (1946). Austin, TX: The Texas Senate.*

Senate Staff Analysis and Economic Impact Statement. (2000). *Senate Bill 68*. Tallahassee, FL: The Florida Senate.

Shea, J. (2003) Percentage plans: An inadequate substitute for affirmative action in higher education admissions. *Indiana Law Journal, 78*(1), 587–618. Retrieved 13 July 2015 from http://www.repository.law.indiana.edu/ilj/vol78/iss1/15.

Solórzano, D.G., & Yosso, T.J. (2002): A critical race counterstory of race, racism, and affirmative action. *Equity & Excellence in Education, 35*(2) 155–68.

Solorzano, D., Ceja, M. & Yosso, T. (2000). Critical race theory, racial microaggressions, and campus racial climate: The experiences of African American college students. *Journal of Negro Education*, 69, 60–73.

Stake, R. (1995). *The art of case research*. Thousand Oaks, CA: Sage Publications.

Starling, G. (2002) Managing *the Public Sector*, Sixth Edition.

State University System of Florida (SUSF). (2014). Interactive university data. "Fall Student Enrollment in SUS Institutions," Retrieved December 8, 2014 http://www.flbog.edu/resources/iud/enrollment_search.php.

Stepping Up the Pace. (1958, 8 Dec.). *Newsweek, 6.*

Stowell, W. (2002) *Biondi v. City of Chicago*, NO. 88C3773. *National Law Journal, 24*,(43).

Subotnik, D. (1998). What's wrong with critical race theory?: Reopening the case for middle class values. *Cornell Journal Of Law And Public Policy 7*, 681–756.

*Sweatt v. Painter*, 339 U.S. 629 (1950).

Swygert, H.P. (2004). *The accomplishments and challenges of historically Black colleges and universities*. 2nd Annual African American Leadership Summit: Washington, DC.

Taking the Initiative. (1998). Retrieved March 26, 2006, from http://www.highbeam.com/doc/1G1:53459607/Taking+the+Initiative.html?refid=SEO.

Taylor, E. (1999). "Critical race theory and interest convergence in the backlash against affirmative action: Washington State and Initiative 200." CEL: Resource Papers. Retrieved June 15, 2015 from http://depts.washington.edu/uwcel/resources/papers/taylor_e_01.html.

Taylor, Aaron N., Diversity as a law school survival strategy (2015). Saint Louis U. Legal Studies Research Paper No. 2015–1. doi: 10.2139/ssrn.2569847.

Tennessee State University. (2006). *History of Tennessee State University*. Retrieved January 20, 2007, from http://www.tnstate.edu/interior.asp?mid=938&ptid=1.

Tewksbury, D.G. (1932). *The founding of American colleges and universities before the Civil War*. New York: Teachers College Press.

The Leadership Conference. (n.d.) Affirmative Action. Retrieved from civilrights.org.

Thomas, K. (1994, February 20). Recalling sad memories of a law school that died or was Stolen. *Tallahassee Democrat.*

*United States v. Fordice*, 505 U.S. 717 (1992).

U.S Census Bureau. (2002). *Current Population Survey.*

U.S Census Bureau. (2014). "Florida surpasses New York to become the nation's third most populous state, U.S. Census Reports." Retrieved from https://www.census.gov/newsroom/press-releases/2014/cb14–232.html.

U.S. Commission on Civil Rights. (1977). Statement on affirmative action. Clearinghouse Publication 54. Retrieved from http://www.usccr.gov/aaction/state77.pdf.

U.S. Department of Education (2006). National Center for Education Statistics. *The Condition of Education 2006*, NCES 2006–071, Washington, DC: U.S. Government Printing Office.

U.S. Department of Education. (n.d.-a). National Center for Education Statistics, Digest of Education Statistics. Based on Integrated Postsecondary Education Data System (IPEDS), Fall 2013.

U.S. Department of Education. (n.d.-b). Programs. Asian American and Native American Pacific Islander-Serving Institutions Program. Retrieved from http://www2.ed.gov/programs/aanapi/index.html.

U.S. Department of Education. (n.d.-c). Programs. Developing Hispanic-serving institutions program – Title V. Retrieved from http://www2.ed.gov/programs/idueshsi/index.html

*University of California Regents v. Bakke*, 438 U.S. 265 (1978).

Valdes, F. (1999). Afterword: Theorizing "outcrit" theories: Coalitional method and comparative jurisprudential experience racecrits, queercrits, and latcrits. *University of Miami Law Review*, *53*, 1266–1322.

Vinson, F.M. (1950). *Sweatt v. Painter* majority opinion. U.S. Supreme Court.

Walker, B.S. (2007). Two states, two stories. Diverse Issues in Higher Education, *24*(3), 15.

Warren, E. (1954). *Brown v. Board* majority opinion. U.S. Supreme Court.

Webb, N. (1981). Task related verbal interaction and mathematics learning in small groups. *Journal of research in Mathematics Education*, *22*(5), 366–389.

Wenglinsky, H. (1996). *The* educational justification of historically Black colleges and universities: A policy response to the U.S. Supreme Court. *Educational Evaluation and Policy Analysis*, *18*, 91–103.

West, R., & Turner, L. (2004). *The narrative paradigm. Introducing communication theory: Analysis and application.* 2nd edition, New York: The McGraw-Hill Companies.

Weston, M. (2005). *The letter from Leon County jail: Patricia Stephens Due and the Tallahassee, Florida civil rights movement.* Unpublished master's thesis, The Florida State University.

White, J. (1992). *U.S. v. Fordice* majority opinion. U.S. Supreme Court.

White House Initiative on American Indian and Alaska Native Education, U.S. Department of Education. Tribal colleges and universities. Retrieved from http://www.ed.gov/edblogs/whiaiane/tribes-tcus/tribal-colleges-and-universities/.

Williams, J., & Ashley, D. (2004). *I'll find a way or make one: A tribute to historically Black colleges and universities.* New York: Harper Collins.

Wing, A. (2000). *Global critical race feminism: An international reader*. New York: New York University Press.
Wolcott, H. (1999). *Ethnography: A way of seeing*. Walnut Creek, CA: Alta Mira Press.
Wolcott, H. (1995). *The art of fieldwork*. Walnut Creek, CA: Alta Mira Press.
Yin, R. (1994). *Case study research: Design and methods*. Thousand Oaks, CA: Sage Publications.

# Index

Page references for tables and figures are *italicized*.

# About the Authors and Contributors

**Adriel A. Hilton**, Ph.D. is vice chancellor for Student Affairs & Enrollment Management at Southern University at New Orleans. Recently, he served as dean of students and diversity officer at Seton Hill University. In the past, Dr. Hilton has served as chief of staff and executive assistant to the president at Grambling State University and assistant professor and director of the Higher Education Student Affairs program at Western Carolina University.

Dr. Hilton was the inaugural assistant vice president for inclusion initiatives at Grand Valley State University. He honed his expertise in higher education administration and teaching at Upper Iowa University (UIU) as executive assistant to the president and assistant secretary to the board of trustees. He was that school's first chief diversity officer and an adjunct faculty member at both UIU and the University of Northern Iowa.

Adriel is a noted scholar. As a Frederick Douglass Teaching Scholar at Clarion University of Pennsylvania, he taught and developed academic programs within the Office of the Provost. Previously, he served as the first public policy fellow at the Greater Baltimore Committee, a leading regional organization comprised of civic and business leaders in Baltimore, Maryland. There he worked closely with advisors to research, develop, and advocate a public policy agenda to advance the organization's work in various areas, including access to health care.

A prolific author and researcher, Dr. Hilton's research is published in refereed journals, such as *Teachers College Record*, *Journal of College Student Development*, *Community College Review*, *Community College Journal of Research and Practice*, *Journal of Applied Research in the Community College*, and the *Journal of the Professoriate*. His numerous service commitments include membership on the editorial boards of the renowned *Journal of Negro Education* and the highly acclaimed *College Student Affairs Journal*.

Dr. Hilton holds a Bachelor of Business Administration degree in finance from Morehouse College, Atlanta, Georgia; a Master of Applied Social Science degree, with a concentration in public administration from Florida A&M University, Tallahassee, Florida; a Master of Business Administration degree from Webster University, St. Louis, Missouri; and a Ph.D. in higher education, with a concentration in administration, from Morgan State University, Baltimore, Maryland.

**Richard D. Schulterbrandt Gragg III**, Ph.D. is professor of environmental science and policy in the School of the Environment at Florida A&M University in Tallahassee Florida. He teaches undergraduate and graduate courses in environmental toxicology, environmental ethics, environmental health, and environmental justice and directs undergraduate and graduate students in thesis and dissertation research. His scholarship, research and professional interests include: environmental health disparities, environmental equity and justice, and environmental science and sustainability. He is published in *Environmental Justice*, *Health Affairs*, *Journal of Environmental Health*, and *International Journal of Public Administration*, and is co-editor of *Environmental Justice Reader: A Survey and Review of Critical Issues in Disenfranchised and Vulnerable Communities in the Twenty-First Century* (Linus Publications, 2012). He is also a contributor to *Sustainability in Higher Education: Stories and Strategies for Transformation* (MIT Press, 2013). He is the founding director of the Center for Environmental Equity and Justice (1998–2011) and a former member of the Audubon of Florida Board of Directors, the Florida Environmental Regulations Commission, and the US Environmental Protection Agency where he served on the National Environmental Justice Advisory Council and the Health and Research Subcommittee. Dr. Gragg received his B.S. degree (1981) in biochemistry, M.S. degree (1986) in pharmacology, and Ph.D. degree (1994) in pharmaceutical sciences from the Florida A&M University.

**Marissa C. Vasquez**, Ed.D. is an assistant professor in the Department of Administration, Rehabilitation, and Postsecondary Education (ARPE) at San Diego State University (SDSU). Dr. Vasquez teaches courses in Community College Leadership and Student Affairs. Her research has focused on three areas. The first involves transfer students and their pre/post transitional experiences to a four-year institution. The second looks at Latinx students in college settings and understanding their experiences from multiple perspectives. Her third research strand focuses on the role of community colleges in creating equitable environments for disproportionately impacted students. Dr. Vasquez is the Associate Director of the Community College Equity

Assessment Lab (CCEAL), a national research and practice center focused on improving outcomes for traditionally underrepresented and underserved students in postsecondary education.

Dr. Vasquez earned an associate degree from Southwestern College in Chula Vista, CA; a B.A. in English from the University of California, Berkeley; a master's degree in counseling with a specialization in college counseling and student development from the University of San Diego; and an Ed.D. in educational leadership from San Diego State University.

**Megan Covington**, Ph.D., is a research associate at Frederick D. Patterson Research Institute at the United Negro College Fund (UNCF). Dr. Covington is a budding scholar in the area of diversity in higher education, honing a content expertise in areas that highlight the strengths and contributions of historically Black college and universities (HBCUs), examine the experiences of African-American women throughout academe, and investigates various aspects of the overall experiences of underrepresented students, faculty and staff from a critical perspective. Dr. Covington's teaching interests focus on student development and critical theory, identity exploration, and qualitative research methodology.

Dr. Covington has facilitated workshops and presentations on topics related to equity and inclusion, as well as authored several publications which have been featured in the *Journal of Multicultural Education, Studies in Graduate and Postdoctoral Education, College Student Affairs Leadership* journal, *Huffington Post*, and *Diverse Issues in Higher Education*. She is also the 2016 recipient of the North Carolina College Personnel Association's (NCCPA) Outstanding Graduate Student Award and the 2017 recipient of the National Association of Student Affairs Professionals (NASAP) Outstanding Graduate Student Award.

Dr. Covington holds a bachelor's degree in psychology with a minor in child development and family studies from North Carolina Agricultural and Technical State University and earned her Master of Education in Higher Education Student Affairs from Western Carolina University. Dr. Covington earned her Ph.D. at the Higher Education program at Indiana University Bloomington.

## CONTRIBUTORS

**William B. Harvey** has compiled over four decades of experience in the academic and non-profit sectors. A distinguished researcher and administrator, Harvey's scholarly activity has been focused on the cultural and social factors that affect underserved populations, with particular emphasis on college and university settings. His extensive list of publications includes books, book chapters, refereed journal articles and professional and technical reviews. Among his recent scholarly contributions are: "Chief Diversity Officers and the Wonderful World of Academe" in the June 2014 issue of the *Journal of Diversity in Higher Education*; a commissioned paper for the Kirwan Institute for the Study of Race and Ethnicity at Ohio State University entitled "Higher Education and Diversity: Ethical and Practical Responsibility in the Academy," and two co-edited volumes, *Footprints to Success in the Academy*, and *Perspectives on Change in the American System of Higher Education*, which were published in both English and Chinese by the Ocean University Press of China. Harvey serves as distinguished scholar at the American Association of Access, Diversity, and Equity, and he is also an executive editor of the *Negro Education Review*; associate editor of the *Journal of Multicultural Learning and Teaching*; and an editorial board member for the *Journal of Diversity in Higher Education*, the *Journal of the Professoriate*, and *Effective Practices for Academic Leaders*.

His previous administrative positions include appointments as dean of the School of Education at North Carolina A&T State University; provost/vice president for Academic and Student Affairs at Rosemont College; vice president for Diversity and Equity at the University of Virginia, where he directed the Virginia-North Carolina Alliance for Minority Participation and secured a five million dollar grant from the National Science Foundation; vice president and director of the Center for Advancement of Racial and Ethnic Equity at the American Council on Education; and dean of the School of Education and deputy chancellor for Education Partnerships at the University of Wisconsin-Milwaukee. He also served as chief executive officer of the International Reading Association. During his career, he has held tenured full professor positions at the University of Virginia, North Carolina State University, the University of Wisconsin-Milwaukee and North Carolina A&T State University.

In addition to having served as chair of the Education Advisory Committee of the National Aeronautics and Space Administration, Harvey has been a visiting associate at the Smithsonian Institution, an American Council on Education fellow, an Institute for Educational Leadership fellow, and a summer research fellow at the Center for Advanced Study in the Behavioral Sciences at Stanford University. He is the founding president of the National Association for Diversity Officers in Higher Education and a past member of the boards of the American Association for Blacks in Higher Education, the National Council for Research on Women, the Yale-Howard Center on Health Disparities, the W.E.B. DuBois Scholars Program at Princeton University, the Study of New Scholars Project at Harvard University, the Site Support for Schools Project at Johns Hopkins University, the Martin Luther

King Living History and Public Policy Center, and the Board of Visitors at the University of Pittsburgh School of Education.

Harvey received a bachelor's degree in English from West Chester University (PA), a master's degree in social and philosophical foundations and doctoral degree in anthropology of education from Rutgers University.

With more than forty-eight years in higher education, **Dr. John T. Wolfe, Jr.** continues to be actively engaged as an academic administrator, faculty member, consultant, and mentor with deep compassion for and commitment to those who seek the opportunities, advantages, and perspectives of higher education.

He has served as president of Kentucky State University and Savannah State University respectively. He has also served as associate vice chancellor for faculty affairs for the 35 institutions in the University System of Georgia. Most recently, he served as associate vice chancellor for Academic Leadership Development and Diversity for the 11 institutions in the University System of Maryland (USM) where he coordinates programs for the development and advancement of academic departments chairs and deans. He is the primary point of contact on diversity issues for the USM.

Highlights of the many professional and civic activities with which he has been involved include hosting "The Educational Forum," a Bowie State University cable television program, and serving in the following roles: president of the Black Caucus of the National Council of Teachers of English, a member of the National Council of Teachers of English Board of Directors, a member of the National Association for Equal Opportunity in Higher Education delegation to West Africa, chair of the Kentucky delegation to a White House conference on libraries and information services, a member of the American Council on Education Commission on Leadership Development, a member of the NCAA Division II President's Council Transition Team, an invited higher education policy presenter at an International Conference on Inclusion in Higher Education in Bellagio Italy, a member of the University System of Georgia Yamacraw Design Center review team in Glasgow, Scotland, and a member of the writing team for the 2014 Maryland State Plan for Postsecondary Education.

Because of his longstanding commitment to service, he has served as secretary and president of the Higher Education Group of Washington, D.C. He has served as a two-term chair of the Washington, D. C. Regional Task Force Against Campus Prejudice (WRTF) and chair of the Historically Black Colleges and Universities Regional Summit on Student Retention. He is a member of the National Association of Diversity Officers in Higher Education.

Dr. Wolfe is a member of the Alpha Kappa Mu and Kappa Delta Pi honor societies. He has held fellowships with the Gulf Oil Faculty Forum, National

Endowment for the Humanities, and the American Council on Education. He has been honored as an old master by Purdue University and was inducted into the Washington, D. C. Urban League's Senior Hall of Fame.

Dr. Wolfe's publications cover linguistics, curriculum, literary criticism, technology, photography, and higher education topics. He earned a bachelor's degree in English-Education from Chicago Teachers College, a master's degree in English-Education, and a Ph.D. in linguistics from Purdue University.

www.ingramcontent.com/pod-product-compliance
Lightning Source LLC
LaVergne TN
LVHW011816200926
848484LV00005B/1213